NO MORE SH*T MANAGERS

Seven steps to a
coaching culture

JO WRIGHT

www.get-known.co.uk

This book is dedicated to the memory of my mum.

She passed away when I was only seventeen years old, and in our short time together she taught me that anything is possible.

There wasn't a day went by without her saying to me:

"There's no such word as can't."

On a side note, it was many years later, when casually browsing through the Oxford English Dictionary that I discovered, contrary to popular belief, that there is indeed such a word as "can't"!

Nonetheless, by the time I had this new insight, my mum's positive intentions behind her sentence were lodged deep inside my heart and mind and have stayed with me forever.

So, when you read this book, I hope you remember this story with a smile and let her words inspire you too.

CONTENTS

THIS BOOK IS FOR...

Leaders who know that the time has come to make a change in the workplace. It's for those leaders who want to make a difference to their culture and put an end to the constant nagging feeling that managers could be better. It's for those leaders who know that coaching conversations are part of the solution but aren't quite sure where to start.

- Do you know, deep down, that work should feel better?

- Do you know that managers should be having better conversations?

- Do you feel unsure how to go about helping them?

- Do you feel like you're getting push-back all too often?

- Do you want to make a real difference but need guidance to do so?

If you answered 'yes' to any or all of these questions, then please be reassured that you're not alone. I wrote this book for you because, throughout my career, I have also answered 'yes' to the above questions. I have spent the last two decades working to help business leaders build their capability and confidence so that they too can make lasting changes in their workplaces..

In fact, I am here for you as a real-life example of how coaching can change lives. Learning how to coach as well as being coached changed everything for me.

"So why does coaching tend to be reserved for a select few?" you may be asking.

A great question indeed.

I am a firm believer that everyone should have access to affordable coaching conversations. I am also a firm believer that given the right support, managers should be the ones who are capable to have those conversations.

If you agree with me, then this book is most definitely for you.

Despite the cheeky title, this book is not for you if you have picked it up hoping it will be some 'manager-bashing' book. It's most certainly not that. It's a book that, if acted upon, will change the world of work for the better and for the long term. It aims to give you hope, inspiration, and practical resources. And I truly hope it serves as a reminder that there's no such word as can't.

THIS BOOK WILL...

Give you a simple framework to help you to build a coaching culture by transforming your managers so they can have more coaching conversations and make a real difference at work.

It will give you all the tools and resources that you need to make this happen.

If you spend the time to read what's in this book and start to take action, then watch the magic happen around you.

You will start to see that:

1. The senior team buys into cultural change.

2. The senior team provides the time, space, and resources for coaching conversations.

3. Managers have the capability and confidence to coach.

4. Coaching and feedback are part of everyday life.

5. Relationships are stronger, trust is built, and business performance improves.

And while you will see, hear and feel a notable difference at work, you will be able to sit back with a wry smile, knowing that you were instrumental in making that change.

Not only that, but this book will take you on a journey that gives you:

1. The comfort and confidence to know that you can do this.

2. The reassurance to know that you are not alone on your journey.

3. A simple step-by-step guide on how to build a coaching culture.

4. Real-world case studies and measurable results to prove that it works.

5. All the tools, resources, practical tips and exercises to make the changes that you desire.

Trust me when I say this, but your frustrations at work will start to disappear, as you feel more energised and valued for the impact you are having, and life in general will start to feel easier.

MEET THE AUTHOR

Who is Jo Wright?

Jo Wright is:

1. The passionate co-founder of the award-winning business, Coaching Culture Ltd, originally founded to ensure coaching conversations could reach the masses, not just a select few.

2. A down-to-earth and engaging cultural change leader who is on a mission to inspire as many people as possible to think differently through the power of coaching.

3. A life-long learner, who believes that every day is a school day.

4. At her happiest when exploring new and beautiful places or reading books that educate and inspire.

5. A firm believer that life is for living, for taking chances and for having fun. All the while remembering that work is an important part of that.

Jo Wright has:

1. Co-founded Coaching Culture Ltd, a business with over 100 digital customers world-wide, that has given tens of thousands of people the resources to build their confidence and capability to coach, while on a mission to make work better.

2. Co-created 'Mindset', one of the world's first self-coaching tools to help people raise self-awareness and change perspective and behaviours for the long term.

3. Spoken to thousands of people around the world to share ideas, challenges, and best practice, dedicated to helping organisations build a coaching culture.

4. Raised thousands of pounds for Cancer Research by running multiple 10km races, one half marathon, jumping out of aeroplanes (not once, but twice…) and bungee-jumping off a 200-feet-high bridge in Northern France.

5. Parachuted from 2,000 feet, unintentionally landing on a marquee hosting the Lakeland Rose Festival, surprising a crowd of elderly folk who were proudly showing off their prize-winning roses. It's worth noting that while this may have surprised them, it did not, however, surprise the people who knew Jo the best…

To contact Jo direct, you can reach her at:

Website: Jowright.com

LinkedIn: Jowrightcoach

HOW TO USE THIS BOOK

Firstly, let's clear one thing up right now.

This book isn't another boring business book. You might have already gathered that from the title.

Let's unpack that choice a little – or justify it, depending on your view.

It came to me when I was busy chatting to people at the Learning Technologies exhibition in London in May 2023. When I told them that our business, Coaching Culture, existed to make work better, they smiled at me warmly. When I told them that we make good managers even better, their faces lit up. But it wasn't until I whispered 'to be honest, we're on a mission to eradicate the world of sh*t managers' that they started to jump up and down before regaling me with story upon story from their own careers. Suddenly it became obvious why this mission was striking a chord.

Taken aback slightly, I took my usual approach and headed to LinkedIn, looking to get the opinion of the masses. The very people who are likely to read this book. And my good friends and followers on LinkedIn told me everything I needed to know. The cheeky title was the right one. I did one more piece of research before I could make my final decision, and that was to ask my 76-year-old dad if he'd be OK with a swear word in the title of my very first book.

His answer?

'As long as it's not the f-word, Jo.'

With that, the decision was made.

So, that's my rationale unpacked and justified. But it's more than the title that makes this book different.

Why?

Because I've written it with purpose and passion, from the heart, sharing decades of practical learnings, toe-curling stories from my career as well as heart-warming case studies. This book will inspire you to realise you can do this too. I hope it makes you smile and grimace in equal measure as the stories resonate with you and, most importantly, equip you to make work better.

The great news is that by reading this book you have everything you need at your fingertips to achieve your goals.

Also, just to clarify some important points:

- Throughout the book, when I refer to leaders, I'm referring to those who can influence organisational strategy, who are responsible for budgetary decisions and who can influence direction.

- When I refer to managers, I'm referring to those who are responsible for motivating, supporting and developing their team. They are the ones having conversations with their team every day. So, for the purpose of this book, a leader could also be a manager of people.

- When I refer to leadership style, I'm referring to the preferred style used to get the most out of their teams.

- Lastly, you'll also find me referring to the People function and People teams, despite some organisations still saying Human Resources. I can't deny it, I don't love the term HR. To me, it sounds a bit cold and dated. Whereas, for me, People function does what it says on the tin. A function dedicated to supporting and enabling the people. A term that feels warmer for sure.

In Part One of the book, I will share personal stories about how this book came about, provide compelling evidence why building a coaching culture matters, introduce the seven step framework to you and cover off any niggles of doubt you may have along the way.

Whereas in Part Two, you will be introduced to more real-life learnings, tried and tested solutions, fresh ideas and resources, all backed up by real-world case studies to help you on your journey to achieve your goals.

As this book is a step-by-step framework helping you to build a coaching culture, I encourage you to read it in the sequence that it's written. There's a workbook that supports the book, for you to carry out simple and practical exercises at the right time for you and your organisation.

With that in mind, I encourage you to head over to jowright. com and download the workbook, carry out the exercises and capture your own reflections. For those who are wanting to go further, you can also head over to coachingculture.com where you'll discover an impressive library of resources, content and premium digital tools.

Throughout the book, when you see the GIFT icon – 🎁 – please let it serve as a gentle reminder that I'm here to help, and that all the resources and tools you need to build a coaching culture have been created for you.

Finally, if you are short on time and want to quickly pick out the hard evidence that building a coaching culture is achievable, please make sure you read the case studies that are covered at each step of the framework. I'm confident that, in time, you'll realise that if others have done it, so can you.

A GIFT FOR YOU

Please visit **www.jowright.com**
to download the workbook and to access a library of
free downloadable content and resources

I WROTE THIS BOOK...

To support as many leaders as possible to make work better, to ensure coaching conversations happen throughout the organisation and to give managers the confidence and capability to do so.

This book will take frustrated leaders from the point where they are struggling to implement the change they know is desperately needed, to having all the tools and resources they require to build a coaching culture that is fit for the future.

I'm delighted that you have made the decision to join me and many others who are on a mission to make work better. You are about to discover a simple framework that will help you to build a coaching culture.

I truly hope that you enjoy the book as much as I have loved putting pen to paper. I hope you enjoy the stories, case studies and resources within this book, so you can take the valuable learnings and make a difference straight away.

Before you dive in, why not download the workbook from jowright.com to assess and map out where you think your culture is right now?

Finally, and most importantly, please have fun and enjoy the journey you are about to embark upon.

PART ONE

CHAPTER 1

TIME FOR CHANGE

GROUNDHOG DAY

Meet Sarah. She's in her mid-forties, she's a wife, a mum of two and a busy senior leader in the People team of a medium-sized charity. She's always worked in HR and People teams. It's where she feels most comfortable – working with people and feeling like she's making a positive difference. She particularly loves the purpose behind the organisation. The charity makes a huge difference to so many lives. And not only that, but her role as a senior leader in the People team also gives her the opportunity to impact many people and their careers.

She wants to enjoy her work, feel like it's truly rewarding and feel valued for what she does. It doesn't seem like too much to ask for. One of the main things she wants to do is to enable managers in the organisation to have better quality conversations. She wants them to get to know their teams, to truly care about them, to ask more questions, to listen more, to build trust with them and to deliver results. Most importantly, she wants it to be done in the right way. She'd love to have the right support, tools and resources to make work a better place for everyone. A culture that everyone can thrive within. Essentially, she wants a coaching culture.

She used to be proud to tell people what she did for a living, and who she worked for. In fact, it used to give her goosebumps whenever she told anyone. Not anymore. Something isn't quite clicking now. She's fallen out of love with the role, and she knows it's because of the inner workings of the organisation. There are obstacles everywhere she looks. From the unnecessary politics to the unacceptable behaviours of some of her colleagues. The long hours, the mounds of paperwork, the never-ending emails, managers who just don't seem to get it, and to top it all off, she has a boss that just doesn't listen. She's dealing with all of this whilst she's trying to implement improvements, leaving her with a constant feeling that she's wading through treacle while climbing uphill. It's all starting to take its toll. No wonder Sarah is feeling jaded and starting to lose the sparkle she once had.

In fact, a typical day for Sarah goes like this…

The alarm goes off at 6.30am, after having had a bad night's sleep – meaning the day is already getting off to a grouchy start. Sarah grabs a coffee and then takes a deep breath; it's time to tackle the first challenge of the day – getting the kids out of bed, dressed, fed, watered and then on to school. All before 8am. Having dropped them off earlier than she would ideally have liked, Sarah heads into work to try to avoid the traffic. Epic fail. The motorway is snarled up. Sarah used to get irritable at all of this and turn up to work like a coiled spring. The years have taught her that it's pointless. Instead, she turns up the volume on the radio and sings along to the 80s tunes that are blasting out. At least it seems to calm her down.

Eventually the traffic starts moving again and, before she knows it, Sarah is pulling into the car park ready to take on the day ahead. It's a busy one. Her calendar reminds her that she's got back-to-back meetings all day. Again.

The morning soon whizzes by, darting between different drab meeting rooms and video calls with colleagues who are working from home. Sarah somehow manages to bounce from a cultural change programme meeting to a one-to-one conversation with her own line manager. Both meetings really grate on her for different reasons. She knows her lack of sleep probably isn't helping, but that is part and parcel of daily life now as her peri-menopausal years are slowly ticking by. The cultural change meeting was like Groundhog Day, having the same conversations about people just not changing their behaviours time and time again. In fact, today it results in a particularly heated conversation with the Head of Operations, or the 'Head of Paying Lip-Service', as Sarah secretly calls him. She then heads straight into a one-sided conversation with her own line manager, somehow ending up with even more tasks to add to her ever-growing to-do list. She needs this extra work like a hole in the head, but she can't bring herself to say anything about it.

It's hardly surprising that, by 2pm, Sarah's rumbling tummy reminds her that she's forgotten to eat. Thankfully, one of her many meetings has been cancelled (at the last minute, as per usual), so she takes the opportunity to grab a coffee and a cereal bar from the vending machine as the work canteen is now shut.

The afternoon continues in much of the same way. More meetings. More conversations. She happens to overhear one of the heads of department cancelling yet another one-to-one with one of their team. This prompted Sarah to question when they'd last had a one-to-one with them. It's been over six months now, apparently. Six months without any focused time with that team member. She silently takes a deep breath to hide this ongoing source of frustration.

Thankfully, and to save the day, Sarah has a one-to-one scheduled with one of her own team. She wouldn't dream of postponing it, despite how exhausted she is feeling. She likes to role-model what she expects of other managers, and spending quality time with her own team is just one example of her approach. It turns out to be a great conversation, leaving them both feeling positive and uplifted. At least progress is being made somewhere in the organisation, she thinks.

Before Sarah knows it, the clock shows 6.15pm, and she is only just shutting down her laptop. She has promised to be home in good time tonight, as the kids have got some friends around after school and she said she would cook their favourite home-made pizza too. She's a good 45 minutes later than anticipated.

Her husband, Chris, and the two kids are used to her saying she'll be home at one time but then appearing at another. Always later than promised, never earlier. It shouldn't have to be that way; it makes for an irritable wife and mum. Sarah doesn't like who she's becoming. No wonder Chris jokingly refers to her as a mood-hoover now and again; after all, she brings her work stresses home with her, sucking up any joy out of their happy family.

Not only is her mood impacting the family, but her friends are noticing it too. Sarah has lost her sense of fun. A glass of wine with her mates used to be a laugh, often resulting in tears of laughter rolling down their faces as they regaled crazy tales about their kids, their partners and the unbelievable stories from their work. Whereas now it's become a pity-party, the chilled Pinot hardly touching the sides as, one after the other, the glasses are downed all too quickly, in between the relentless moaning about the daily grind of life and work.

All of this is stopping Sarah from fulfilling her true potential as a wife, a mum and a senior leader. Becoming the irritable wife that she never wanted to be, the nagging mum constantly having a go at the kids, and the frazzled leader in a People team means that both her positive attitude and confidence has been chipped away. The result is that all of this is leaving her feeling both trapped and burned out.

THE COST OF A TOXIC CULTURE

Sarah isn't alone working in a culture where managers are just too busy to focus on their people. Where it's deemed quicker and easier to just tell others what to do to get the job done. Where getting to know their teams as real people, not just taskmasters, is seen as alien. Where moaning and gossiping becomes the norm. Where negativity is rife and where trust is rock bottom. In other words, a toxic culture.

It's a huge problem for organisations, this constant pressure for managers to be productive all the time. To add more and more onto their to-do lists. To take on more responsibility. To rush from meeting to meeting, from video call to video call. No wonder they are getting anxious, stressed and burned out.

In fact, the C.I.P.D. Health and Wellbeing report (2022) stated that over 79% of organisations in the UK had experienced stress-related absence in the previous 12 months, stating Covid, heavy workloads and management style as the top three reasons for these absences. Shocking statistics in anyone's book.

As part of my role, I get to speak with hundreds of business leaders. Most of them are saying the same thing: they are working in a culture where they are utterly exhausted. Where their managers are just too busy to coach their teams. Where it's quicker to instruct rather than inspire. Where there's too much pressure to get results, and where senior leaders aren't buying in to the need for better conversations. It's a constant battle that's taking its toll on many organisations and the people who work within them.

In fact, toxic cultures are costing the UK economy over £15bn per year, according to Breathe H.R.'s The Culture Economy report, 2021. Furthermore, according to a report by The Society for Human Resource Management in 2019, toxic cultures were estimated to have cost the US economy over $223bn in the previous five years alone.

The importance of culture has never been more real. Since the pandemic, people are simply no longer prepared to accept this type of workplace culture. More and more people are re-evaluating what truly matters, not only at work, but in life. It's hardly surprising that this new awakening was coined the 'great re-evaluation'.

The cost of not focusing on workplace culture will continue to run into the billions. Loss of talent, low engagement levels, poor customer satisfaction, cost of absences, cost of recruitment and onboarding. Not only does it impact organisations but the overall economy too. It is estimated that it costs the NHS over £30billion a year as the overall mental and physical health of the population declines. And while we spend nearly a third of our time at work, it goes without saying that it impacts most areas of our lives.

Whoever created the phrase 'work/life balance' has a lot to answer for. They were clearly implying that work and life are like two separate loads on a weighing scale that need careful monitoring. When one gets more focus than the other, the other loses out and ends up becoming out of balance. It doesn't have to be this way. They are not separate loads on different ends of a weighing scale; work is an intrinsic part of our life. Therefore, having the opportunity to work within an enjoyable culture, where people feel listened to, valued and where they can unleash their full potential, surely has to be the answer.

US AND THEM

It's hardly surprising that Sarah and many others have such challenges in their organisation. For many years now, managers have been expected to have all the answers. To be seen as the boss, the boss's boss, the boss's boss's boss, the ones that are looked towards for clarity and direction. To have their capability reaffirmed as the fountain of all knowledge and wisdom, without which they would be showing vulnerability and incompetence. And not only that, but if they didn't have the answers, then who would?

It goes back to the 50s and 60s, when the old school 'command and control' style took hold, following the industrial revolution and two world wars. It was a time when our grandparents and parents were in employment, often working for only one or two employers throughout their whole career. Going in every day for hours on end, to only take a measly wage home at the end of the week. Employees were expected to do as they were told, to follow orders within the hierarchical structure. Questions weren't asked, opinions and new perspectives weren't valued. The decisions were made at the top, and that was that. It created a culture of 'us' and 'them' where both workers and bosses were following orders. Adherence to inflexible policies and procedures was paramount.

This style of culture and leadership has been passed down over the years, and it is another reason why Sarah is still feeling the pain. The constant tension between the old and the new; Sarah feels like she's in the middle of some weird game of tug of war. A tension between old school ways, where leaders bark orders and pull out the hierarchical card when needed, versus the more refreshing styles of the newer generations.

She seems to be getting bogged down by people who don't want to acknowledge that there is another way. They are resistant to change. They aren't seeing the value in changing the culture. They aren't prioritising better quality conversations or actively listening to the new kids on the block. They've got their tried and tested way of doing things, so what's the point anyway? Especially when there are way more pressing priorities within the organisation. Just another change that is doomed to fail.

Fundamentally, Sarah knows that many of them are simply stuck in the past. It's making it a damn sight harder for Sarah when her own line manager is one of those who is stuck too. With aspirations to leave the business in the not too distant future, Sarah's line manager has no desire to embark on a journey of personal change any time soon.

With all that history, internal noise and challenge, no wonder Sarah is frazzled, exhausted and questioning so much. The odds seem to be firmly stacked against her, especially as evolving a culture is like moving an oil tanker: it's slow and it takes time. However, the great news is that it is possible. When you start small, make one move at a time, it all starts to become achievable.

A COACHING CULTURE

Now some organisations embark on a cultural change programme by allowing the senior leaders to stand up and just tell everyone what they're going to do, what they're going to change and then leave them to it. They somehow expect the changes to magically happen. Even more so, they suddenly expect their people to be experts in change. They bring together special task forces or attach 'transformational change' onto someone's already busy role, without giving them the tools and support to enable change.

They recognise that to change culture, impacted teams will need new capabilities, so they scramble together just enough budget to send certain teams onto courses to acquire new skills. However, further on down the line, they look back and wonder why cultural change just isn't coming to fruition.

Changing a culture and the way people behave for the long term doesn't just happen overnight. It's not a case of waving a magic wand, ticking the 'training' box, or telling people to just change. It runs way deeper than that.

While cultural change is hard, it is possible and, in most cases, necessary. The organisations who will thrive in the present, and in future decades too, are those that will listen to the needs of a new generation, the leaders of tomorrow, and strive to meet them.

I am fortunate to be able to speak with many leaders who face similar issues to Sarah, and while some are at the start of their journey towards creating a coaching culture, some are already there. They are the ones who are winning. The ones who are attracting the talent, who are developing their teams, retaining the best people, winning awards, and achieving their strategic goals.

Helping organisations to make work better and inspiring people to think differently through the power of coaching is what I do. Helping organisations to realise the benefits of a coaching culture by transforming their manager conversations is my absolute passion. My reason for being.

Why? Because I've seen too many people over my 30-year career who have experienced transformational results by having outstanding managers who have used more of a coaching style. Being coached and learning how to coach others was certainly life-changing for me. It may sound dramatic, but it's true. That's why I am happy to shout from the rooftops at every opportunity to share the multiple benefits that a coaching culture brings.

"

A coaching culture is a
place where authentic
leaders and managers
help people to grow, thrive
and perform through
effective conversations
and honest feedback,
underpinned by trust.

"

CHAPTER 2

MY STORY

MY INNER IMPOSTER

I've always worked hard, harder than the average Jo. No matter what I set my mind to, I always throw myself in fully. I have been the one working the longest hours, the one going the extra mile, the one secretly craving recognition from others for my efforts. I certainly don't wear it as a badge of honour because it's not. I quietly get on with it, pushing myself harder and harder. In fact, I'm even writing this chapter now at 5am on a Saturday morning while the rest of the world sleeps. It's in my DNA. The constant need to be on it, achieving, pushing myself, feeling like I'm doing something worthwhile.

It started at school and has carried through into my adult years. Some would call it 'the good girl syndrome': when females feel that they must achieve something incredible to gain any recognition. I now know it as something else. It's imposter syndrome, through and through.

How has this shown up for me in my career? In so many ways, actually.

As an example, I think my personal favourite is the fact that I've often had roles that have meant I've had to commute for over two or three hours just to get to the office to see my colleagues. I'll never forget the time when I was due to leave the office early so that I could make the four-hour drive for a Valentine's meal that my husband was preparing for us. As soon as I turned onto the familiar motorway, my heart sank. It was just bumper-to-bumper with cars and lorries. We were all going nowhere fast. I fell through the door at 10pm that evening. I'd probably say that my 'dinner was in the dog', but we don't have a dog. I'm hoping you're catching my drift. It was certainly a memorable Valentine's evening, but for all the wrong reasons.

The constant racing around the country like my backside was on fire just left me feeling utterly exhausted, but it was never enough to stop me. It never made me wonder if there was another way to live my life.

THE REDUNDANCY BOMBSHELL

It was a crisp November day, back in 2015, and I was making my regular three-hour commute to London by train. There was nothing strange about this, as far as I was aware, I was just heading to the corporate head office for a team meeting. I always enjoyed going to London. Being a Northerner, it always felt like I was a bit of a tourist, even though I was there to work. From first stepping off the train at Euston to arriving at the office, I just loved the London vibe. Watching everybody rushing from meeting to meeting, absorbing the hustle and bustle of it all. Equally, I was in awe of those who were sitting outside the cafes, sipping their favourite frappuccinos, catching up with friends and just chilling. I always wondered how they found the time. Did they not work? Why were they not as busy as me? Nonetheless, I would breathe in the atmosphere and try not to stare at strangers in awe at how cool they all looked. It was just so very different from the small Northern town that I grew up in, which happened to be known more for its industrial-aged cotton mills than its cutting-edge fashion.

I arrived early for the team meeting, as usual. The meeting went well, and I felt like I contributed plenty of ideas and suggestions. In fact, I was the only person in the room who had not worked in the People function all my career. I personally saw this as a positive, as I could comfortably put myself in the shoes of others, having worked in many of the roles that the People function was there to serve. Some of the People team members liked to say that I'd worked within the business. It was a reference that always concerned me. In my opinion, we were all working in the business, all on the same side. To some, it was a normal part of their language. To me, it implied a culture of us and them, and that just felt alien to me.

My inner imposter was well hidden on this day, and I was feeling confident about how things were going for me in the organisation. I liked the team I was working in, and I enjoyed my role. I'd only been in the business for two and a half years and was thriving on the challenge. With the exception of a few numpties here and there, I genuinely enjoyed the people I was working with. One thing I particularly loved was the feedback that I was getting along the way. I was getting regular praise from my internal stakeholders as well as my own team. It was the fuel that gave me the energy to keep on going with the crazy commutes and the endless meetings. I was doing a pretty decent job and making a difference. Or so I thought.

There was nothing unusual about this team meeting. It came to an end mid-afternoon, as expected. I know that because I was carefully watching the clock as my train from Euston was only hours away. There was nothing worse than having to hot-foot it across London at rush-hour, only to be met by hundreds of tired commuters on the station concourse eagerly waiting for the platform number to be announced. I had a meeting scheduled with my manager to talk through the structural changes we were thinking about. I knew that I didn't have hours and hours to talk it through, so I quickly headed into her office armed with my proposals and plonked myself down.

In the event, I didn't need much time. My manager had very different ideas about the outcome of the meeting. Unbeknown to me. She interrupted me quite early on as I was busy presenting the potential team structure going forward, where I'd put myself firmly at the top of the structural tree.

I can't remember the exact words that were spoken. It's all a bit of a blur even to this day. The top and bottom of it was that I wouldn't be part of the team going forwards. My manager had a different structural proposal to present, and not only was my role changing, but my role was being made redundant.

WHATTTTTTTTTTTTT??????????????????

Well, that bombshell certainly wasn't in my plan.

I was then presented with the redundancy figures and had a brief chat before being sent on my way. Job done.

Literally.

Off I went back to Euston for the three-hour commute wondering how the hell I was going to tell my husband that our income was now in serious jeopardy.

I bumped into a neighbour of mine on the train. Weirdly, this had never happened before, considering it was such a popular commuter route. I started to spill the beans about what had just happened. I was still in shock. Devastated, in fact. I'd never been made redundant before. Yet here it was, happening to me for the very first time as I was fast approaching my 44th birthday. My neighbour listened carefully and compassionately as I just rambled on and on until I had to come up for more air.

What have I done to deserve this?

What would people think?

How would I pay our mortgage?

What was I going to do next?

Those were just some of the questions that I was asking as I travelled home with my poor neighbour, who was undoubtedly regretting the fact that he'd bumped into me on the train. He'd also had a tough day at work and probably wanted to talk about it too. Nonetheless, if we were playing 'tough day top trumps', I was winning hands down. So, with that, he slumped back in his seat and listened.

In the weeks that followed, I felt utterly broken. Struggling to make sense of what had happened and what was to come next. For the first time in my career, I suddenly had time to spare. I could have met up with the friends I'd not had a chance to see for years. Instead, I remember feeling lost and lonely, and I allowed the days to pass by aimlessly.

As time went by, the emotional wounds that this self-confidence battering experience had given me started to heal. I decided to dust my trainers down and began to run again. And this time it wasn't across station concourses, it was out in the fresh air, giving myself a physical and mental workout. I remember listening to the song 'Things can only get better' by D-ream. I started to cry while out on that run. 'I bloody well hope so,' I thought, 'because this situation is making me feel like shit, and I don't do "feeling like shit" very well.'

I knew I had to make a change, and it had to start with me. I remember thinking to myself, *I will never, ever let anyone control my career in this way again.*

It was the best lightbulb moment I ever had.

THE START OF PERSONAL CHANGE

One of the first things I did was attend a networking group. It was a bit of a random decision and not the sort of event I would ordinarily throw myself into. But there I was, unemployed for the first time in my career, figuring out exactly what I was going to do next.

I got chatting to a couple who recommended that I should attend a training course led by a local entrepreneur who they both knew well. It was a course intended for self-employed individuals and business owners who wanted to learn how to sell their knowledge in the form of online training.

'Why not?' I thought. 'I'll give it a go. I've got nothing to lose.'

The entrepreneur was a guy called Adam Kara, the then CEO of Learning Heroes (now Litmos Heroes). He took a bit of convincing to get me onto his course, because I was neither self-employed (yet) nor a business owner (yet). Somehow, I managed to convince him that it was the right decision to let me onto his course and I gate-crashed my way in.

One sunny Saturday morning in January 2016, I drove to the hotel in Warrington, taking in all the fancy Range Rovers that were parked outside. I took a deep breath and walked into the training room. My inner imposter was having an absolute field day. As we sat in the typical U-shaped layout, we went around the room and introduced ourselves one by one. It was a slow, creeping death by awkward introductions.

It felt like an age before it was my turn.

'Hello, my name's Simon, and I run a group of dentists.'

'Hello, my name's Tim, and I have a chain of accountancy businesses.'

'Hello, my name's Amanda, and I've got my own marketing business.'

15 more business owners introduced themselves, then it was over to me. 'Here goes,' I thought, and I took a deep breath… 'Hello, my name's Jo and I've recently been made redundant.' There, I said it, it's out there now.

What happened next blew my mind.

Everybody started to clap and cheer.

Have I missed something here? Has someone famous just walked through the door? I thought.

Apparently not.

There were more shouts of woo-hoos and well dones.

WOW!

Now that's not what I was expecting. Until that point, everybody else I'd spoken to about my new situation had commiserated with me. In fact, they'd talked to me in such a way that I felt like the end of the world had arrived.

In that very moment two things dawned on me:

1. I wanted to surround myself with such positive, entrepreneurial people with an unlimited growth mindset.

2. I wanted to set up my own business.

The next thing I did when the redundancy cheque landed was to enrol on a coaching course. I wanted to achieve both a post-graduate qualification and a leading accreditation in the coaching market. It was something that I had been wanting to do for years, but I'd never found the right time or money to do it. While I'd always been someone who had coached my teams, and I knew the massive value of coaching, the real lightbulb moment came when I was a Change Manager on an organisation-wide change programme. I saw with my own eyes that people don't just magically change when they're told to. They need more than that. They need to be engaged, to be asked their opinions, to be heard and understood. Most importantly, they need to be bought in to the change. It was clear to me that there was something way deeper going on. It had everything to do with psychology, the inner workings of the human mind and behaviour. To me, it was simply fascinating.

I was now clear in my mind that I wanted to set up a business to help organisations through change and to help managers learn how to have better conversations. The problem was that I didn't have a clue how to set up a business. This was hardly surprising as I'd worked in the corporate world for well over 20 years where everything was pretty much set up.

I was riddled with fear.

Full of self-doubts.

Could I do this?

It wasn't only me that was feeling fearful, my husband was too. He was worried that we wouldn't have the same income as before to pay the mortgage. Worried that we'd have to sell the house and change our lifestyle dramatically. I needed his affirmation that I'd be good enough and that I would succeed. It wasn't overly forth-coming. The odd comment here and there wobbled me and made me question whether I was doing the right thing. I understood his position completely, but I knew I had to at least give it a go. I didn't want to get to the age of 60 and have any regrets. I was definitely in the mindset of having a go and failing miserably, rather than not having a go at all.

But how could I overcome such crippling fear and start to believe in myself again? It was not easy for someone who had carried a rucksack of boulder-sized limiting beliefs around on her back all her life. Or at least that's how it felt.

So, while I was learning how to coach others, I was also being coached by the other trainee coaches who were equally practicing their new coaching skills.

I decided to take only one important challenge to be coached upon.

'Can I go self-employed?'

Let me share the life-changing moment when the answer came to me.

I was being coached by Caroline, one of my fellow trainee coaches who I had instantly warmed to. She was way more experienced than me. She was already a successful business owner herself, and she had the knack of making me feel safe. It was one of those walk-ing and talking coaching sessions in the great outdoors. It was a beautiful day. The sun was shining, the birds were chirping in the trees and there was a gentle breeze in the air. We were strolling around the beautiful Derbyshire village, racking up our daily steps when I started to share all my fears.

'What if I fail?'

'What will other people think of me?'

'What about my husband?'

'What about our family?'

Caroline stopped dead in her tracks. I did too. I turned to face her and held my breath. I even think the birds stopped chirping too because we all knew she had something important to say.

'You are brilliant. Absolutely brilliant. The only thing that is getting in your way is YOU,' she boomed.

CLINK.

The penny suddenly dropped. It was like it had been stuck in my throat for a lifetime, and suddenly it dropped into my stomach.

'She's right,' I thought. 'It's not about anyone else. It's me, I'm the only one getting in my own way. I CAN do this.'

I felt shaken and a bit tearful but certainly overjoyed, like a dark cloud had lifted. She was so right. I wanted to hug her. I knew that something very special had just happened.

I embarked on a mission to set myself up in business as a self-employed Change Consultant and Coach. I'll always remember the very first day that it was officially all down to me, and only me. I literally couldn't get out of bed. I don't mean in the luxuriating way that says, 'I deserve a lie in'. This was different. I felt crippled with fear. Hiding under the warmth and security of the duvet while the rest of the world went around their normal business felt like the best option. I had nothing to get up for. After a while, I had a harsh word with myself and gave my head a good wobble.

'Get a grip,' I thought. 'If others have done this time and time again, then so can you, Jo Wright.'

HOW TO BE A PEOPLE GURU

I busied myself with all that setting up a business entails. Business name, brand logos, website designs, an accountant, and a bit of a sketchy plan. I started to tell the world what I was up to by announcing it on Facebook and LinkedIn. The response was phenomenal, and the calls of 'do you do this?' and 'do you do that?' soon started to come in. Thankfully, I'd been advised to always answer 'yes' then figure it out later.

'Google will become your best friend, Jo,' I was wisely advised.

My first large piece of self-employed work was an absolute joy. The call came in enquiring as to whether I knew someone who could potentially help an SME with their people strategy as they were going through a lot of change. 'They're looking for a People Guru' were the exact words. I sat and thought long and hard about all the names in my little black book of People Gurus, wondering who could help this fabulous business. It suddenly dawned on me that that person could be me. While I wouldn't have exactly described myself as a self-confessed People Guru, I had plenty of experience in behavioural change, change management and leadership development to get them started, so I threw my name into the hat and quickly googled 'How to be a People Guru'.

I launched myself into this piece of work in typical Jo style and I absolutely loved it. It still fills me with joy when I think about that business, the people within it and the success we had together embarking on the cultural change programme. By now, I was a professionally accredited Coach, so not only were they getting Jo, the newly self-employed Change Consultant, they were getting the freshly qualified Coach, desperate to put my new skills to good use.

I could see and feel the impact I was having as I worked with the business. I often liken the role of being a cultural change leader to that of a conductor of an orchestra. Gently conducting different areas of the orchestra at different times, while the cymbals will be crashing in one area, the flutes will be sweetly playing in another. The role of the conductor is to bring the musical harmony together, just like the cultural change leader who seeks to engage and unite. One conversation at a time.

I never imagined that my coaching qualification was going to be so personally life changing. I always imagined it would be about me becoming qualified to help others to release their potential. When in fact, it allowed me to release mine too. It helped me to recognise that we have untapped potential within all of us. It allowed me to dig deep into the psychology of the mind, the importance of mindset, why we do what we do and how to change for the long term.

While I was busy enjoying my self-employed life, something then happened, totally out of the blue.

One Friday evening in early 2017, I received an unexpected message from Adam Kara, the local entrepreneur whose course I'd shamelessly gate-crashed only twelve months earlier. He mentioned to me that he'd moved to the village where I lived. Apparently, he knew where I lived because he'd spotted me checking in to the local wine bar on Facebook one too many times. Not exactly what I wanted to be known for, but hey ho. Shit happens.

'Where exactly have you moved to?' I enquired, out of politeness more than anything. He shared the name of a small cul-de-sac on the edge of the village, assuming I wouldn't have a clue where it was.

'Do you drive a black Range Rover?' I asked, as I remembered all the fancy cars outside the training course.

'I do,' he said, probably now worrying where this was all going.

'You've just moved next door but one to me,' I declared.

THE BIRTH OF COACHING CULTURE LTD

Over the following months we started to chew the fat about business as I eagerly picked his brains as an already successful business owner. One evening, while sat putting the world to rights, Adam asked me what organisations were really needing. I thought long and hard and then answered, 'sustainable behaviour change'. We then went on to talk about how too many organisations were focusing on developing skills and knowledge, whereas real change came about when mindset and behaviours were addressed.

I told him that learning how to coach, and being coached too, had been life-changing for me and that it was shocking how it had taken until the age of 44 for me to suddenly realise all the things that had been holding my life and career back. We discussed how, if coaching could change one person's life, maybe it could change the lives of many others too. The problem was that coaching seemed to be reserved for a few people at the top of the organisation which, quite frankly, seemed morally wrong. And if organisations were wanting sustainable behaviour change and coaching conversations were the answer, then we had to figure out how to help as many of them as possible to build a coaching culture.

We turned to our mutual best friend, Google, and searched the words 'coaching culture'. While the odd academic paper popped up here and there, not much else did. Rather than being put off by this, we knew that there wasn't only a gap in the market, there was a huge gaping hole staring us right in the face.

We just had to figure out how to fill it.

And so, it began.

In the summer of 2017, the business that is now Coaching Culture Ltd was officially born. From a blank piece of A4 paper, with a few scribbled ideas on it, we set about growing a community of people who thought the same as us. They knew that coaching was the answer, but needed the tools, resources, support and solutions to help.

To check just how many other people were thinking the same as us and to share ideas and stories with them, we started off by creating a magazine. Granted, it wasn't the most obvious place to start, but it was certainly innovative and fun.

'You're going to have to be the editor of the magazine,' said Adam.

Hang on a minute, I thought…

'I've never been an editor of a magazine before,' the imposter in me nervously replied.

'Well, you are now,' he replied.

That was the quickest recruitment I've ever been involved in, I thought, as I went to find my big girl editor shoes to go and step into.

Thank goodness I did, because I absolutely loved it.

Putting together the first magazine was such a great feeling. Having the opportunity to work with such brilliant people, on such fascinating topics that could help organisations to think differently, was a joy.

I'll never forget the moment when Adam and I received the very first issue of the magazine. We sat on the floor, handwriting and stuffing about 200 envelopes to send out to the people who had raised their hands to say they too were interested in building a coaching culture.

Over time, more and more people started to join our growing community. They wanted access to our content and resources, and to connect with like-minded people. It soon began to snowball as growing numbers of organisations started to talk about needing a coaching culture. I felt privileged to be able to speak to a growing number of inspirational people in organisations who thought like us. They knew that coaching was the answer but didn't have a clue how to go about bringing it to the organisational masses.

I'd already commented to Adam how it seemed criminal that professional coaching tended to be reserved for a handful of the most senior leaders in organisations, and how such a potentially life-changing solution should be made available to everybody. This got the cogs whirring in Adam's entrepreneurial brain.

I'll never forget the moment he asked me whether coaching could be done digitally. I was just about to blurt out 'no way, it's a human thing' when I stopped and thought it through. Coaching is fundamentally about asking powerful questions, allowing people to self-reflect to help them to think differently and change behaviours for the long term. So, after some thought, I answered with a firm 'yes' instead.

And I'm delighted that I did.

Because, with Adam as the digital entrepreneur and me as the Coach, we knew we had the joint capability to create scalable digital solutions to help organisations, and that's what we set out to do.

A number of months later, our first digital self-coaching solution was born, and we called it Mindset.

I could talk for hours and hours about the journey we've been on. The ups, the downs, the funny moments, the not so funny moments, but I'll cut a long story short for fear of losing you.

For the first time in my life, I felt like I was starting to do something worthwhile, providing valuable content and resources, while inspiring as many people as possible to experience the benefits of a coaching culture.

Nonetheless, it soon became apparent that neither my kitchen table nor Adam's home office were cutting it. We also knew that we weren't going to be able to achieve our growth ambitions with just the two of us. We founded our first office above a small dry cleaner's shop in our local village and set about recruiting our first employee, then the next, then the next, then the next.

From something that started out as a deep conversation, putting the world of organisational development to rights, the business has now developed into something very special. We now have thousands of people all over the world accessing our resources and using our solutions. Our customers range from small charities to large private organisations. The one thing that they all have in common is this: they all want to make work better. They are all on the journey to ensure that their teams develop greater self-awareness, and where their managers have better conversations, give honest feedback, and build trust to ultimately drive business performance every single day.

The benefits that our customers talk about include improving their employee engagement, wellbeing, inclusion, confidence, resilience and so much more. And they know it's because the cultural tide is slowly turning as their managers recognise the impact of their courageous conversations and the importance of self-awareness. They tell us how our solutions are not only providing lightbulb moments here and there, but they are also illuminating the way forward, setting the cultural tone for today's employees and those of the future.

CHAPTER 3

A DOSE OF THE YERBUTS

Y ou may still be thinking, 'Yeah, this all sounds well and good, Jo, but I'm just not sure a coaching culture is right for my organisation right now.'

I totally empathise with you. Change isn't easy, but it is necessary to move us forward. Without change, you'll stay stuck in your old ways or, worse still, stagnate like a millpond, with nothing fresh flowing in or out. There's nothing more inevitable in life than change. So, rather than burying your head in the sand and hoping it will all happen organically and without some effort, it's time to think again. It's time to get stuck in. While I can empathise with those who resist or fear change, it also prevents so many people from getting out of their own way, stepping out of their comfort zone and making huge strides. It's outside the safety of our comfort zone where the magic happens, after all.

These are some of the thoughts you might be having right now, or worse still, you may just be experiencing a serious dose of the 'yerbuts'... they're a bit like hiccups, but the words 'yeah but...' are spoken out loud and in quick succession!

"Yeah, but Jo, it's not the right time. It's just not a priority at the moment. We're really busy, there are more pressing areas to address in the business right now than building a coaching culture."

OK, I'd like to throw something your way for you to mull over. If building the capability of your managers to have better conversations (because you know they're already having conversations every single day) is not pressing right now, why not ask yourself what you actually consider to be pressing right now. Ask yourself this: would managers adopting a coaching approach to those strategic priorities make life easier? I bet, after some quiet reflection, the answer would be 'hell, yeah!' Building a culture where conversations and feedback are higher quality and more effective will help you to achieve the rest of the business priorities. The organisations that are well on their way to building a coaching culture are already seeing and feeling the business benefits.

'The time isn't quite right' was a common objection before the pandemic. That all changed when we had to suddenly pack up the office and work from home. Some of our potential customers were kicking themselves as they recognised the value in managers being able to support their teams from afar. Our phone started to ring with concerned employers hastily enquiring about our coaching solutions.

"Yeah, but Jo, it's just going to be too hard. I'm already wading through treacle here. I've got to really win people over, get their buy in, show them the art of the possible and then make it happen. Changing the culture in my organisation is not going to be for the faint-hearted."

OK, you're right. It won't be easy, but it is possible. Doing nothing won't change the culture. And it won't change overnight. One small step forward in the right direction is as good a place as any to start. While this book and the case studies within it will help guide you along, inspire you with ideas and motivation to keep you making progress, remember the necessary resources have already been created to support you. You're not alone in this. The ideas and inspiration are all here in this book from those who have been there, done it, and are now proudly wearing the t-shirt.

To help you, you'll meet Michelle, one of our superfans and our very first customer, later in the book. She will happily tell you that working with Coaching Culture gave her the confidence and the resources to bust any internal myths and prove beyond any reasonable doubt that building a coaching culture makes a commercial difference and that it's most definitely worth it.

"Yeah, but Jo, unless I can show the ROI of coaching, my senior team, and especially my Finance Director, will never buy into it."

The ROI of coaching. An emotive yet interesting topic for discussion. It reminds me of the story of when Gary Vaynerchuk, the famous entrepreneur, is asked about the ROI of social media. After some deliberation he threw the question back and asked, 'What's the ROI of your mother?' (Take a look on YouTube if you want to check it out.) OK, so while that feels like a slightly cheeky response, I knew what he was getting at. Sometimes, it's hard to say, 'we spent X and, as a direct result, this is the return on that investment'. That is especially true where cultural and behavioural changes are concerned. But there's more and more evidence out there now to show the benefits of building a coaching culture and the link to commercial success. Done well, there's a return on investing in your people to have better conversations. A better question would be to ask what's the cost of not doing it? I know to us it seems obvious, but it isn't always as obvious to those holding the purse strings.

Interestingly, this question used to pop up a lot before the pandemic. It's hardly asked at all now. Why? Because social media is flooded with stories about the importance of culture and the difference that managers make in an organisation.

"Yeah, but Jo, our managers haven't got the time to coach, so what's the point?"

Aaah, that old chestnut. This is where the age-old discussion about time versus priorities is valid. We all have the same 24 hours in a day. It's how we choose to spend that time that matters. It's time to bust the myth that coaching conversations must take extra time in the working day. They don't. Conversations can take place in two minutes over the water-cooler, five minutes on a video call, or an hour in the virtual office or the warehouse. It doesn't matter.

The conversations are already happening. It's about making them better quality and more effective. It's about managers understanding what makes their people tick, building rapport, developing trust and delivering results.

I'll never forget the moment when Claire, one of the managers who uses our solutions, realised that if she coached her teams more, rather than giving them all the answers, she would not only help them to develop, but she would grow too. She'd always assumed that she was supporting them best by serving up the answers all of the time. Little did she realise she was creating a culture of dependence, and nobody was winning. It was a beautiful moment when a very important lightbulb was firmly switched on.

"Yeah, but Jo, we're too much of a fast-paced, high-pressured environment to be able to coach."

I get it. I understand. I too have worked in fast-paced environments where slowing down to stop and think was simply seen as 'not working'. This is where the phrase 'slow down to speed up' springs to mind. I know it sounds counter-intuitive, but it's a proven technique; when we slow down our racing mind, we are more creative, more productive and we improve our performance. Slowing down to have better conversations will ultimately speed up the results in the short and long term.

Nonetheless you know:

- That employees are wanting a different style of leadership these days

- That managers have a significant impact on the employee experience

- That there are multiple benefits to building a coaching culture.

So surely it's time to connect these dots and make the changes you want to see in the organisation?

If you have any more concerns, bat them my way, because I will send them back every single time. It'll be like a game of tennis, and I will win, game, set and match. Now don't get me wrong, I do understand that change can feel difficult. The alternative of staying put or, worse still, going backwards is often unimaginable.

I truly hope by now that I have opened your eyes to the art of the possible. To believe in yourself, knowing that you can do this. Let's face it, if others have embarked on this journey and are succeeding, you can too.

So, why not make a start today?

CHAPTER 4

THE FRAMEWORK

THE SEVEN STEP FRAMEWORK

In this chapter, I'll introduce you to our simple framework to help you create a coaching culture. It'll take you from not knowing where to start, or from feeling frustrated about not seeing the results you want, to having the tools and resources you require to build a culture that is needed now and in the future. You'll learn what it is, where it comes from, why it works and who it works for. I'll share how our customers use this framework to help overcome the lack of senior level buy in, improve managers' capability to have better quality conversations and create a coaching culture that builds trust and high performance.

It's a simple, step-by-step guide to inspire you to think about how you can unlock and harness the collective potential within your organisation. Afterall, there'll undoubtedly be a lot of untapped potential kicking about, just waiting to be released. So, I want this framework to get your cogs whirring, prompt new ideas and assure you that there is a way through the somewhat crazy maze that is otherwise known as cultural change.

What is it not?

Well, it isn't one of those overly complicated processes with more twists and turns than an Agatha Christie novel. Nor is it steeped in rich sentences that leave you begging the question, 'why use twenty words when you could have used one?' It's not that either. It'll be straightforward, to the point and simple to understand. Sounds like heaven, right?

So let's make a start. The framework has seven steps. Let me explain why.

Seven is a memorable number, that makes me think of world class leadership books, such as Stephen Covey's *The 7 Habits of Highly Effective People* or Michael Bungay-Stanier's *The Coaching Habit*, which includes seven essential coaching questions.

The first two steps are very much the 'thinking' stages. The final steps are the 'doing' stages. The first two steps of the framework are:

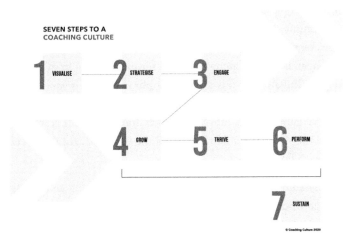

While the steps could look like a straight road to success, we all know that change doesn't happen like that – it's just not a linear process. Some organisations start from step 4 or 5, then they go back to step 1when enough evidence is gathered to prove the case. Others start at step 1. It all depends on the individual organisation and what will work best for yours.

Change can often feel like two steps forward and one step back, and that's OK, if you stay connected with why you're doing it and what your vision for the future is. If you want to achieve greater business results for your people, then the most important thing to do is to simply start somewhere.

If this is what you want, then this framework is most definitely for you.

NO MORE 'INITIATIVITUS'

But first, you're probably wondering where it came from. Well, it's been bubbling away in my mind for many years. It really started to bubble to the surface when I was a Change Manager, focusing on the people strategy for a large-scale transformational change programme. I had previously worked in businesses where I had seen many a change initiative fail… and when I say 'fail', I don't just mean little blips along the way, I mean, bombing from a great height. 'Initiativitus' was a common phrase in the organisations that I worked within. As initiative after initiative went through the cycle of launch, train, move on, launch, train, move on. It used to make me shudder thinking about all the time and cost that went into each failed effort.

It wasn't until I moved from being on the receiving end of the change initiative to being part of a hand-picked project team, whose sole purpose was to implement large scale change, that it became clear to me that there were many different dynamics at play. I don't mind admitting that I struggled with the role at first, because I had always previously had roles that had a clear input and output. If you did this, the result would be that. This felt different. It *was* different. It wasn't just a case of simply telling people to change and, hey presto, they did. This was more about carefully conducting an orchestra. I was looking to win hearts and minds to allow people to buy into the change, providing the right support, development and environment for the change to happen and for people to flourish.

I was fascinated by what I was seeing and hearing. I knew that there was more to enabling change than met the eye. As I started to dig deeper and deeper into supporting the changes, I felt like I'd discovered the best kept organisational secret to success. Imagine accidently stumbling upon the secret recipe to Kentucky Fried Chicken. It was just like that.

So, over the past decade, and building on a career of over 30 years, I have managed to speak with many people, studying the best in the world, understanding challenges, frustrations, what works and what doesn't, and bottle the secret to success in this framework. I am so excited to be sharing it with you. Getting this right will set you and your organisation up for the future, enabling you both to achieve your goals and vision of success.

A SIMPLE FRAMEWORK

The difference with this framework is that it's simple and practical. It's based upon years of experience, of being curious about successes and failures, but most importantly, it's based upon the desire to make a difference to the world of work. That's why I do what I do. I have a burning desire to make work better and to inspire people to think differently, not only for today's employees, but for the workplace that our own children and grandchildren will encounter.

The framework could simply focus on the 'doing' part of the process, building up the capability of a few managers dotted around here and there, which would get pockets of results. The difference with this framework is that it reaches the very core of the organisational culture. It considers the 'thinking' required to build organisational habits that create lasting change.

When people work with Coaching Culture, they don't expect us to come in, wave a wand and magically make everything better. We form a partnership where we both do our fair share of the work. Every organisational strategy is different after all. While one size doesn't fit all, this framework shares best thinking, which can aid and guide you on your own specific journey.

We have a brilliant team whose sole purpose is to work with our customers to help them build a coaching culture and optimise the use of our solutions to reach their goals. The great news is that our customers come back year on year and give us glowing feedback to say how our team and our solutions are helping them to achieve success. We're forever grateful for the relationships that we form and the difference we are making. For both of us, it's an evolutionary journey, rather than a destination. As the world never stops moving, neither shall we. Instead, our customer success will drive us, like rocket fuel, to reach more people across the globe.

NO ROCKET SCIENCE REQUIRED

This framework works for frustrated leaders who are struggling to know where to start, or find themselves wading through treacle, but who want practical tools and resources to build a coaching culture. Sounds all too familiar, right? It also works for those who don't consider themselves experts in change, or those who have been part of the 'Initiativitus' brigade in the past. That's OK, as long as you bring the rich learnings, the highs and the lows, from past endeavours with you to this fresh approach.

Furthermore, you don't need to be a qualified coach or have a PhD in rocket science to make this work. Not at all. This *isn't* rocket science. This is about being curious about people and about what makes them tick. Even more than that, it's about being passionate about making a difference to the people at work and the culture that they work within. What I need you to bring to the party is a true passion and a commitment to making a difference. That's it. In a nutshell.

FRAMEWORK IN ACTION

This takes me onto the story of Michelle, the Director of Performance, Culture and Delivery at the Institute of Occupational Medicine, a UK-based research charity and consultancy. You may remember me mentioning Michelle in an earlier chapter. She is one of our superfans and the first official customer of Coaching Culture. Michelle joined her organisation back in 2018. She soon identified that the nature of the business had created a culture that was old school and institutionalised, one of getting your head down and getting on with the job, and that was it. The culture was broken, and the people were disconnected from their own purpose and the purpose of the organisation.

As a result, the balance of conversation was definitely in favour of technical tasks rather than people. The people were a great bunch. They loved what they did but felt way more comfortable in the technical space than in the 'thoughts, feelings and behaviours space'. Michelle could see the size of the cultural opportunity and the difference that a more people-focussed culture would make to the conversations and the results of the business.

She knew in her heart that the answer was to create a coaching culture.

She had a vision to create a culture where people felt valued, where they saw how they delivered value and where they knew how they received value. Developing a culture where both behavioural and technical capabilities were rewarded would be central to this.

To be able to do this, she started to open up a new type of conversation throughout the organisation. She needed to get an accurate sense of where the culture was at. So, in her earliest of days, she not only set about connecting people at all levels together, but she also started to reconnect them with the purpose of the business. She saw her role as the 'enabler of the employee voice', the person who asked powerful questions, listened with intent, and built trust. An out and out 'People Warrior', in my opinion.

She knew what she felt in her heart wasn't enough. She needed evidence to back it up, so she started asking simple but powerful questions such as:

"How does it feel to work around here?"

She had countless individual conversations and focus groups, asking people to share their stories about what was working and what wasn't, which started to reconnect them with the organisational purpose.

When she'd gathered enough evidence, Michelle set about convincing her peers and colleagues that things needed to change if the business was to succeed. This meant conversations at the most senior level to get the required buy in. She knew that this was going to be a significant change to the way the organisation had been operating. It wasn't going to happen overnight. Yet the business results still needed to come in. This was not a straight-forward goal, but it was one that Michelle was determined to achieve, knowing it was the right thing to do.

The first place Michelle started was with the board, who she considered at the time were fundamentally broken. She needed to get alignment and buy in to her vision, and did this through the power of her own coaching conversations. It's hardly surprising that she had countless sleepless nights worrying about these conversations, when the mirror was going to be firmly held up to them as individuals and as a group, relaying what the people were saying.

Some of the conversations didn't land as well as she would have liked. Afterall, she was a relative newcomer to the organisation and here she was beating a shiny new drum about cultural change, people development and employee value.

Nonetheless, with an unwavering resolve, Michelle carried on with her conversations. Every bit of her knew it was the right thing to do. As time went on, she won more and more of the boardroom over, resulting in her getting the buy in she needed to make the organisational changes.

BOOM! What a result.

Soon the time came to win the hearts and minds of everyone else, getting the organisation to feel excited about the way forward. To quote Michelle, she 'jazz-handed her way through her daily role.' While it was both exhilarating and exhausting, it only took a matter of six months for the results of the employee voice to increase by 60%. How? This took nothing more than asking, listening, and acting on the organisational insight. The secret sauce had been there all along. It was just quietly hidden deep within the heart of the organisation. Deep within the people.

Something special started to happen.

The leadership team were listening, and trust was growing at a rapid rate of knots.

No wonder I felt genuinely honoured when Michelle reached out to ask me if I would attend a strategy day to deliver mini-workshops with the aim of inspiring the masses about building a coaching culture. She wanted me to share the numerous benefits and leave them safe in the knowledge that a coaching culture was the answer. I was delighted to pack up my soapbox and head to beautiful Edinburgh so I could inspire a group of highly intelligent technical people about why a coaching culture mattered.

Michelle also wanted me to share how the Coaching Culture solutions would help people to develop their mindset, own their own development and build their capability to have better conversations. Like many change initiatives, it was recognised that, if our solutions were rolled out too widely, too soon, it would be coined as just another fad (remember 'Initiativitus'?). So, instead of launching with full whistles and bells, they started small. Michelle made the solutions widely available, and people were signposted to them. The solutions were also blended into management one-to-one conversations. It wasn't long before the impact of the solutions started to be talked about more and more, and the benefits were promoted by the people themselves via their intranet. Michelle started to see a fabulous ripple effect throughout the organisation.

The digital coaching solutions were more than proving their worth. This helped Michelle to secure more funding for a leadership development programme to further grow people's capabilities to have better conversations. She introduced more face-to-face coaching solutions to provide a total blended approach and, before she knew it, 'coaching champions' began popping up all over the place as the impact of coaching conversations started to take hold.

Michelle also provided tools for teams to raise their team awareness, and she constantly communicated the importance of coaching conversations through her own words and actions. To keep the conversations truly alive, and in response to organisational feedback, Michelle ditched the annual appraisal system in a blaze of glory and implemented a system to capture everyday coaching conversations and feedback.

Nonetheless, the true impact of this hard work wasn't fully felt until the pandemic hit. While the rest of the world scratched their collective heads and wondered how to navigate through the crisis, Michelle describes this time in her organisation as 'too easy' because the culture had already started to shift. The people were now fully supportive of the leadership team, people were communicating and collaborating beautifully, and she knew her vision was becoming a reality. The pandemic simply accelerated the strategy that was already in place.

Today she beams with pride when she shares how they are making significant progress with their coaching culture. Not only are people developing and growing personally, but conversations are becoming more and more people-focussed, not just technical and task-based.

'What about the commercial results?' you may be asking.

Well, that's when Michelle really lights up. Through unleashing the value of their people, the business has delivered the strongest commercial success in its history.

It's hardly surprising that Michelle is a huge advocate and trailblazer for the difference a coaching culture can make. Her positive impact gathers her more and more fans along the way. Her no-nonsense yet wonderfully warm approach to sharing best thinking has meant that she has gone on to be named one of the top three HR Directors in Scotland in 2021, and one of 'HR's Most Influential Practitioners' of 2022, which is one of the most highly acclaimed accolades within the HR industry.

> *"The ongoing support from Coaching Culture has been amazing. The team are always on hand to help; they check in regularly and share any new developments, resources, and best-practice that continue to help us on our journey. They always take the time to understand our needs and wants. I am a huge advocate of the Coaching Culture platform and the services that the Coaching Culture team provide the business world."*

**Michelle Reid, Director of Performance,
Culture and Delivery,
Institute of Occupational Medicine**

SEVEN STEPS TO A COACHING CULTURE

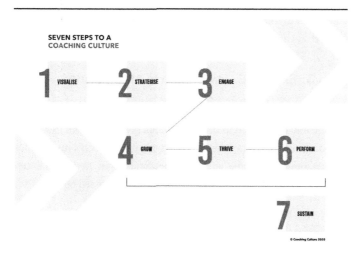

SEVEN STEPS TO A COACHING CULTURE

1 VISUALISE — 2 STRATEGISE — 3 ENGAGE

4 GROW — 5 THRIVE — 6 PERFORM

7 SUSTAIN

© Coaching Culture 2020

Step 1: VISUALISE – start with the end in mind

For a coaching culture to develop, the senior leadership team must be able to visualise and articulate the culture that they want to see, hear and feel in the organisation. They need to fully buy in and be able to lead by example.

I'm going to share how you can get their buy in, and how you can demonstrate the benefits, so that they provide the time, space and resources for better quality conversations to happen every day.

Step 2: STRATEGISE – define the strategy

Everybody needs to be clear what is going to happen, how it's going to happen and when. A strategy that will take the idea from a concept into reality is the key to being successful. This needs to happen before the wider business can be fully engaged.

I'm going to share how a coaching culture needs to align with organisational goals, values and the expected behaviours in the business. Furthermore, I will share the actions that need to be considered so that the cultural change can be sustained.

Step 3: ENGAGE – win hearts and minds

To build a coaching culture that lasts, everybody needs to be excited about it and committed to making it happen. It's important to demystify coaching and define what it is, and what it isn't, to encourage better conversations. This is the 'winning hearts and minds' step. A vital step when implementing change, and often one that is missed out.

I'm going to share how you can engage the wider business to ensure coaching and feedback become part of everyday life.

Step 4: GROW – grow coaching capability

When managers are having better quality conversations, the magic really does start to happen. This is about reassuring managers that they can do it and giving them the time and space to make it happen. I'm going to share the different ways that you can enable your managers to have a coaching conversation and ensure that they have the confidence to have a go.

Step 5: THRIVE – unlock the power of feedback

To establish a strong coaching culture, coaching conversations and feedback must become part of everyday life. Feedback is one of the most powerful and cost-effective development tools and often one of the most untapped. I'm going to share the different methods that you can use to ensure feedback becomes the expected and respected way of communicating.

Step 6: PERFORM – build trust and drive high performance

It's no surprise that better conversations and relationships build trust, and in return, high trust builds high performance. This step is all about ensuring that better conversations become the way to communicate and to manage performance. It's a myth that building a coaching culture is separate from managing performance. The two go together. I'll show you how to redefine performance management and replace the archaic annual appraisal system with everyday conversations and feedback.

Step 7: SUSTAIN – embed a coaching culture

To embed the behavioural changes so that coaching conversations and feedback are happening day in and day out, this step is all about ensuring managers are role-modelling quality conversations and are giving and receiving feedback. I'll share with you the different ways that have worked for our customers to embed the cultural change.

There you go. A whistle-stop tour of what this framework is going to help you to achieve. By now you should be realising that it is possible. It's been done by many organisations and, most importantly, you can do it too. This framework will give you the confidence to have the necessary conversations in your organisation. To convince the cynics and the naysayers that it is the right way forward, and just as importantly, to convince them that you have the tools and resources to get started.

So, that's it. Part One of the book is done.

You're hopefully getting a sense by now that I'm passionate about helping you on your journey. Well, the next part of the book will show you how. This is where I will guide you through the framework, step-by-step, sharing real world stories, inspiring case studies and practical exercises to get you going. If you haven't done so already, remember to access your free gifts to set you on your way.

I suppose the only coaching question to pose right now is this:

What are you waiting for?

PART TWO

CHAPTER 5

VISUALISE

Start with the end in mind

"

The true sign of
intelligence is not
knowledge but
imagination.

"

ALBERT EINSTEIN

FRANK BY NAME, FRANK BY NATURE

I was invited to coach the CEO of a medium-sized tech company. Let's call him Frank for now. Frank by name, frank by nature.

Not only that but it became clear over time that he was a CEO who liked to lead with the Frank Sinatra classic 'My Way' in mind. You know the type. The ones who understand one way and one way only, and that's their own way. Others may have called him narcissistic.

Frank had decided that they were going to build a coaching culture. As far as he was concerned, the organisation was already part way down the intended track, or so he thought.

'Jo, I've just had enough. I had a meeting this morning with one of the People team. She was showing me this briefing document she'd drafted. It was supposed to go out to the wider team on our proposed changes. It was really frustrating, to be honest. I had to take it home, spend half the night re-working it until it did the job.'

That was just one of the jaw-dropping moments I've had over the years with board members proudly telling me that they're building a coaching culture. This conversation was with Frank. It was clear he felt he had all the required skills to do every job in the business, and his attitude of 'nobody does it as good as me' permeated throughout every interaction he had. It was his decision to want to build a coaching culture. He'd been to a conference where he'd heard several inspiring stories about the benefits of a coaching culture. He returned to the boardroom and simply told the rest of the board that it was the answer to their prayers. It was how they were going to transform the culture.

Further conversations with the leadership team simply confirmed that they were indeed a business in chaos, largely driven by the 'it's my way or the highway' CEO. Nonetheless, upon firm instruction, they went about trying to build a coaching culture in the best way that they could. When I say 'they', what I really mean is the People Director and his team, not the entire operational board. They made the schoolboy error of assuming that 'culture' was purely down to the People team to fix. They hadn't even agreed as a board what they wanted to see, feel, and hear around the organisation, how it would fit with their organisational values, or how they were going to bring it to life. They were simply acting on Frank's instruction, starting from the position of 'tell' not 'ask'.

Not the greatest foundation for a coaching culture, I hasten to add.

One of the first steps they chose to take was to ensure the middle managers had some coaching skills, while the board and senior leaders were each gifted a book about coaching. The books racked up to a grand sum of £70 plus postage and packing. That was the level of development bestowed upon the most senior leaders. That was the level of thinking that had gone into building a coaching culture.

I kid you not.

It's hardly surprising that this is a snippet from a conversation between two of those middle managers during a coaching workshop.

'I don't even know what I'm doing here,' said one agitated line manager.

'Apparently we're building a coaching culture,' replied another.

'Are we?' he replied with a confused expression.

'Yes, I only know because my boss has been asking me questions taken from his new coaching book.'

It was clear that the board and senior team had simply not agreed or articulated what they wanted from a coaching culture or how they were going to get there. There was a lack of depth in the thinking at this stage of the process, which resulted in a confused team of managers, wondering what they were even doing and, more importantly, why they were even doing it. A common mistake when enabling any form of change.

THE BOARD ON BOARD

It's fair to say that culture can be a tricky concept to define and difficult to change. It includes the subtle unconscious actions and behaviours of everyone within the organisation. It's the unspoken rules, or put simply, the way things are done around here. More than that. It affects the senses. Something that can be seen, felt and heard. When you've got a great culture, it's a truly wonderful place to be. When you haven't, it can feel like hell on earth.

Visualising the future is all about the board getting really clear on what they want the culture to be like going forwards. Before they can do that, they really need to get a clear understanding of where the organisational culture is now. Only when they understand their starting position, can they define the gap to achieve the future vision. They can then set about defining the strategy and take the required actions. Without a clear vision that the board have all bought into, and without them signing up to the fact that they will need to be role-modelling the required behaviours every single day, the rest becomes much harder. While organisational culture is everyone's responsibility, the leadership team play a significant role in setting the tone. People throughout any organisation look to the leaders for clarity, for inspiration, for the norms, so how the leaders go about their daily business becomes part of those accepted norms that others will follow.

STEERING THE TITANIC

Ensuring the board can visualise and articulate the future they envisage is particularly important if you want to embark on cultural change. It's their responsibility to communicate the vision, to inspire and engage the organisation with the way forward. More than that, it's their role to set the tone that builds the trust that underpins any organisational success.

When they are bought in, and truly understand what it will mean for the future, only then can they start to get their heads around how to make it happen. Afterall, if you don't know where you're heading, how do you know where to start?

Another important reason why the board need to be fully supportive of the desired culture is so they can lead by example. They can communicate the message consistently, role-model the necessary behaviours and showcase what is and what isn't acceptable. None of this 'do as I say, not as I do' style of leadership.

There's nothing worse than working somewhere that proudly displays organisational values (or in more recent times, the organisational culture codes) only to see members of the board strut around like they are exempt from the agreed behavioural standards. They set the tone. Loud and clear.

It's becoming more and more commonplace for culture to be placed at the very heart of the organisational strategy. Something that was once reserved for the CEO or the People team is now becoming a core role of the entire leadership population. And quite rightly so. It's too critical a part of the organisational success to place in the hands of one person or one overstretched team. Culture is everyone's responsibility.

When the board can describe the culture that they're striving for, only then can they start to align it with the organisational purpose, values and strategy. You may be asking, 'But which comes first, culture or strategy?' A great question, and an age-old debate. The answer is neither and both: they are inextricably linked and rely on each other to succeed. The strategy being the 'what' and the culture being the 'how'.

I'll never forget having a conversation with an Operational Director, who I'll call 'Mr BS' for now. We were talking about the cultural change programme that the organisation was heavily investing in. 'It's all BS,' he whispered behind his hand. 'We'll never pull this off. It's like trying to steer the Titanic away from the iceberg.'

The alarm bells started to ring loudly inside my head. If I'd have had a bag full of red flags at that moment in time, I'd have pulled them all out and waved them frantically in front of his face. But of course, I didn't. I listened carefully, then probed him further about his distinct lack of belief. He gave me several reasons why it wouldn't be possible and why it, quite simply, would not work.

It was very clear to me that the board had not invested enough time and energy in getting themselves aligned as a group before communicating their intentions to the rest of the business. They should have gone round that loop time and time again until they were all fully supportive. Instead, they had at least one bad apple who was paying lip-service to the cultural agenda. And if he was saying that to me, it begged the question: what was he saying to his team?

THE BOARD NOT ON BOARD

If you don't take the time to get the board on board, then you'll only achieve so much. You won't be given the time, space, or resources for coaching conversations to even happen. And you can't change a culture and expect coaching conversations to become part and parcel of daily life without enabling the organisation to do so. It'll undoubtedly leave you feeling more frustrated than ever, questioning why you're even bothering.

Not only that, but without the board's support, you'll be left scratching your head, feeling bemused and looking around wondering why cultural change just isn't happening. Remember, the impact of the board and the leadership teams runs deep. They set the tone for others to follow. Without their support and role-modelling of the desired behaviours, there will always be that underlying feeling that you're wading through treacle.

Now, having said all of this, some organisations have very successfully begun the process of building a coaching culture at step four or five, building coaching and feedback capabilities. They start small, then go further into the organisation over time. They grow the coaching and feedback capability of their managers first, then gather enough positive evidence and internal feedback to go back to step one. They can then confidently prove to the board that this needs to be a wider organisational movement, not just a capability programme for a handful of people.

Like I said in an earlier chapter, change isn't linear, and what works for your organisation, may not work the same for another. Every organisational strategy is different. This framework is simply here to guide you along the way and to ensure you can pick out the nuggets that work for you and your organisation.

CASE STUDY: INSTITUTE OF OCCUPATIONAL MEDICINE

Back to Michelle, the Director of Performance, Culture and Delivery at the Institute of Occupational Medicine, a UK based research charity. Back in 2018, she was faced with an aging workforce with no real succession plans. Organisational growth and development of the people was stagnating. There was a lack of trust and psychological safety. Innovation and creativity were non-existent. People were fearful and jaded. In fact, they were stuck in a culture that was simply broken.

Michelle knew she had a job on her hands to make the necessary cultural changes, so she asked herself an important question:

'How can I mobilise and accelerate culture change in an affordable way?'

Michelle looked to her external network and came across Coaching Culture.

We had a conversation to discuss the deeper challenges of the cultural change. It soon became clear to Michelle that she needed to think about getting her board members bought into her vision for the future. So, she plucked up the courage and shared with the board the data and insights that she had been gathering along the way.

'This is what our people are telling us,' she declared.

It made for uncomfortable listening and couldn't be argued.

She pressed on and shared her vision of where they needed to get to. Not only that, but she was able to confidently share a proposal on how to get there, thanks to the knowledge and expertise she had gathered from the conversations she had been having with her network and her teams.

After many conversations and facilitated workshops with the board, she helped them to visualise what needed to be done, allowing her to breathe a deep sigh of relief. The next challenge on the journey to cultural change was to help the organisation visualise it too.

She invited me along to a strategy day in a beautiful hotel in Edinburgh. The day had been designed to help the people re-connect to the organisational purpose and visualise what a changing culture could achieve.

My brief was to inspire them to visualise what a coaching culture could look and feel like so that they would engage and drive the strategy forward. I remember feeling a combination of excitement and nervous energy as I joined group after group to talk about the power of a coaching culture, and how our solutions would help them on their way.

As each group joined me in my allocated meeting room, I could feel a ripple of positivity and intrigue starting to take hold. Old concerns were being aired and challenged, as the baton for cultural change started to be handed over to the very people who could make the difference. I could sense the multiple lightbulb moments being switched on as the baton for cultural change was accepted.

Getting the board to buy in to building a coaching culture, and then having the whole organisation follow it, felt like a sizeable win for Michelle. She was now fully empowered to fix the broken culture. Still, to this day, we at Coaching Culture are proud to work with the Institute of Occupational Medicine and see the progress that is being made, as the team there firmly stick to their vision to build a coaching culture.

"You gave me the confidence to take the steps I needed, enabling me to have a conscience and a coach on my shoulder when I needed it the most…"

Michelle Reid, Director of Performance, Culture and Delivery, Institute of Occupational Medicine

WHAT TO DO

Step 1: Determine the current cultural state

To be able to start to visualise a coaching culture, it's important to take a step back and understand what is currently going on in the organisation.

When I work with organisations to help shape their cultural strategy, I ask several coaching questions. Here are just a few examples:

- What does it truly feel like to work in the organisation?

- What are the accepted behaviours and norms?

- How much are the senior leaders trusted?

- What are the employee surveys saying?

- What insight can you take from these?

- What are the people metrics saying?

A good place to start to truly appreciate what people are honestly thinking and feeling is to organise listening groups. It is a great way to spend time with as many people as possible from different areas of the business and ask some insightful coaching questions. The power is listening to what is said as well as what's not said. If you're doing these yourself, it's as important to observe body language as it is to listen to the words that are being spoken. This is a relatively simple but more time-consuming way to get a view of the organisational climate. To complement listening groups, you can also think about investing in a survey tool to create your own organisational pulse surveys, or if budgets allow, invest more heavily into a third-party employee engagement survey. Other data that will support your understanding include people metrics, such as employee turnover, absences, and talent retention.

Before you know it you'll soon start to get a picture of what's going on inside the minds of your people. The data will tell a story.

Step 2: Gather the evidence to take to the board

Now that you've gathered the evidence about the existing state of the organisation, from listening groups, employee surveys, pulse surveys, and the people metrics, it's time to share the insights with the board. Share what the people are currently thinking and feeling, share the stats and evidence that can be used as a spring-board for change. Even if this is a case of moving from good to great, there will always be opportunities for improvements. There's growing evidence out there to show that culture is one of the most critical success factors in an organisation today. Not only that, but there's a growing number of case studies demonstrating the benefits, the outcomes, and the difference a coaching culture can make. Whenever I am asked about this, I recommend people to look at our resources and to download the 'ROI of a coaching culture', a compelling presentation to help sell the story.

Data and insights are important for those sat around the table who are hard-wired to need facts and figures. They're the ones asking 'so what?' at every stage. It's important to leave no stone unturned when you share the case for a coaching culture.

Step 3: Define where the organisation wants to get to

Once you've started to whet the appetite of the board, either bring in an external facilitator or utilise the skills already in-house to deliver a visualisation exercise to them. Let the board imagine the future. Be as creative as possible to free their minds so that they can create a vision of what the culture could be like. It's all about imagining the art of the possible because, as Walt Disney famously stated, 'If you can dream it, you can do it.'

Share what the expected behaviours and actions would be from leaders, teams, and individuals in a coaching culture, and how it will help them to achieve the overall organisational strategic goals. Let them imagine the positive impact of regular conversations that focus on building trust and high performance, and what those conversations would look like. Leave them feeling inspired to create this ideal place to work and get their commitment to start to make it happen.

A positive way to help the board to visualise what success would look and feel like also includes providing coaching support for them. Not only will this help to demystify coaching and remove any negative connotations, but it will also unlock further growth and potential around the board table. This could include one-to-one coaching or team coaching, or both. When the coach-matching is done correctly, this is a brilliant way to prove to the board that coaching conversations work. If they then start to realise the benefits themselves, as a group or as individuals, they can start to visualise how that would translate on a large scale across the organisation. And let's face it, that's when the magic truly starts to happen.

If the board experiences coaching conversations for themselves, they will also recognise and identify what a powerful conversation looks and feels like. They will be able to start to demonstrate and role model the art of asking questions and listening with an empathetic ear. If the board are bought in to creating a coaching culture and are prepared to live and breathe it themselves, then you're out of the starting blocks and on your way to a coaching culture.

EXERCISE: NOW IMAGINE THAT

Visualisation exercises have been around for many years in sport and, thanks to a deeper understanding about the power of the mind, they are now becoming increasingly popular in the business world.

This exercise will ensure the board can visualise a coaching culture, allowing them to articulate what they want the culture to look and feel like in future years. It may prove uncomfortable for some board members who prefer to focus on the here and now. Nonetheless, it's an important exercise to take some time to imagine the future. It's intended to stir up positive emotions, so create the space for the board to sit and reflect in silence.

Ask the board to close their eyes and visualise ten years from now, imagining the following…

Step 1: Visualising success

- Imagine the board together at the Coaching Culture awards ceremony, as the organisation has been nominated for 'coaching culture of the year'. The presenter announces the organisation as the winner of the award and starts to list all the winning accomplishments. Ask the board to think about all the different measures of potential success.

- A video starts playing with a group of customers talking about the organisation, and what it's like to work with them and why they would be a worthy winner of the award.

- Think about what matters to the customers, the quality, the products, the service, the reliability, and what they may be saying.

- A video starts playing with a group of employees talking about the organisation, sharing what it's like to work there and why it should be a worthy winner of the award.

- Consider the things that truly matter to employees and what they may be saying about the culture, behaviours, manager support, personal development, and what it feels like to work there.

Step 2: Stir up emotions

Now let the board take a moment to think even deeper, imagining the following:

- What that successful organisation will look and feel like to them personally.

- What it will mean to them as an individual and to their personal success.

- What it will mean to their family when the organisation is thriving.

Ask the board to sit for a while and think about the emotions this would stir up.

Step 3: Time to share

Now ask the board to open their eyes and share as a group:

- What they saw in their mind.

- What accomplishments had been achieved.

- What customers were saying.

- What employees were saying.

- How it made them feel.

Step 4: Pull it all together

- Now as a group, discuss their reflections and the most important points that they agree upon.

- Collectively articulate what they want the future culture to look and feel like.

 HEAD TO JOWRIGHT.COM
TO DOWNLOAD MORE RESOURCES

TOP TEN TAKEAWAYS

In this chapter, we have learned that:

1. Culture is the subtle unconscious actions and behaviours, the unspoken rules, and the way you do things in a given place.

2. Change isn't linear, so what works for your organisation may not work for another.

3. Organisational culture is everyone's responsibility, so talk to your teams to help set the scene.

4. The leadership team play a significant role in setting the cultural tone.

5. Visualising the future culture is key, as the board need to understand where the organisational culture is right now.

6. To get the board on board and to buy in to a coaching culture you must make sure you gather compelling internal and external evidence to demonstrate the need.

7. The board must be able to articulate the future vision and communicate it in a way that inspires and engages the rest of the organisation.

8. The board must be able to role-model the necessary behaviours.

9. The board must provide the time, space and resources for coaching conversations.

10. The board must be encouraged to experience the benefits of coaching.

CHAPTER 6

STRATEGISE

Define the strategy

"

———————————————

A goal
without a plan
is just a dream.

———————————————

"

BRIAN TRACY

BACK TO SQUARE ONE

'**W**e're going to have to go back to square one,' Tracy said with her head in her hands. She was the People Director of a small manufacturing company. She looked totally crestfallen. She was a warm, quietly spoken woman with a strong, calming presence. She was well on the way to helping transform the culture of the organisation and was doing a pretty fine job of it too. The people and culture metrics were heading in the right direction; attrition was down, employee engagement was up, talent attraction and retention were on track, and the business was having a more profitable year than previously.

I wasn't quite understanding the issue.

'One of the board members is just not getting it. He's saying one thing, but doing another...'

'How do you know?' I tentatively enquired, slightly anxious as to what the answer might be.

'I've had a grievance submitted about him. He's just not living the values we've agreed. And I wouldn't be surprised if more grievances were on the way...'

'Go on...' I gently encouraged.

I stayed silent, so she could explain further.

'It sounds like there's a case for bullying to be honest. Shouting at team members, belittling them in public, undermining them. The list goes on.'

I let out a deep sigh. I just couldn't understand it. All the feedback so far on the cultural work had been nothing but positive. This was not how it was supposed to be. In fact, it was the stark opposite.

'What's making you think you need to go back to square one? This sounds like one rotten apple. Not an organisation-wide issue,' I said, wanting to encourage her while willing it to be true.

'Yeah, you're probably right, but I know exactly what we've forgotten to do along the way, and that's what's probably causing this.

'We've not really got everyone aligned with what is expected when we say, "we're building a coaching culture".

'While the board have all agreed it's the right thing to do (we've agreed what the organisational values are and we've put the resources in place to upskill our managers), what we haven't done is bring it all together. We've not fully aligned the cultural expectations with the business strategy. They've been done separately.'

Now, it was her turn to let out a deep sigh.

I listened carefully.

'This wouldn't be happening if we had got the board really clear on what a coaching culture means, what the behaviours are and what they're not, and more importantly, what they need to do to role-model and embed it.'

I couldn't disagree with that. She was right.

'So, what do you want to do now?' I asked.

'Well, firstly, I need the grievance to be investigated fully. I'll cross the next bridge when I come to it. But it does feel like I need to bring the board back together to agree what we want to see, feel and hear differently in the organisation, and all sign up to what it means to the way we behave too. No ifs, buts or maybes. They also probably need their own coaches too.'

'That sounds like a great next step,' I reassured.

'But first things first,' she said. 'I've got a grievance to resolve.'

CULTURE OR STRATEGY?

There's no point in setting out on a journey without a clear direction and a plan in place to show how to get there. Imagine booking an amazing family holiday, having a beautiful destination to go to, then jumping in the car, dishing out the sweets, then saying to everyone, 'I have no idea how to get us there'. Can you imagine the chaos?

It's the same with culture. It needs a clear strategy on how you're going to get there, and it needs to align with the overall business strategy. Afterall, it's the culture of the organisation that will determine whether the business strategy is achieved.

Just let that sink in.

It's the culture of the organisation that will determine whether the business strategy is achieved.

Now that's powerful.

Roll up the behaviours of every single person in the organisation that create the daily norms and voila! There you have it. The culture is right there before your very eyes.

So, to create a coaching culture, it's not difficult to see that everybody needs to be clear what it means to them and how it will work in practice. And not only does that include the board, but it starts with them too.

This step is all about defining the coaching culture strategy to ensure that all the right actions and measures are put in place to get there. It ensures that the board provide the time, space and resources for coaching, and they clearly understand and can demonstrate the part that they need to play.

It's the practical step that gets into the nitty gritty of what needs to be done and when. It not only sets out the steps that need to be taken to create a coaching culture, how it will align with the organisational values and behaviours, but it also includes how the cultural change will be sustained. To achieve the culture that you want, the expectations about how more conversations need to adopt a coaching style must be articulated at every stage of the employee life cycle. Or, to use a well-known phrase, from cradle to grave. Remember also that technology, systems, and processes all help to sustain and embed change, but more on that later.

WHAT GETS MEASURED, GETS DONE

Ensuring you have a strategy in place to help create and shape the culture is particularly important for business leaders as they are the ones who the organisation looks towards to lead the way. They are the standard-bearers who role model what is expected and respected.

To have a clear strategy in place means that you will have the senior-level buy in and support that is essential when wanting to create a coaching culture. You will have a clear roadmap and budget in place to achieve the things you want to do. It will help you to communicate the way forward and guide the decision-making along the way. It provides clarity of direction.

If the visualisation step was the 'north star', the stated vision of what you want to achieve for your culture, this step is the compass, the map, the fuel and the team that will get you there.

Having all these in place will give you the confidence and know-how to move forwards. The spring in your step will help you to know that you are on the right track. Most importantly, you will have the full backing of the powers-that-be to do what needs to be done. It will allow you to communicate the way forwards with passion and purpose, knowing that you're doing the right thing and you have a clear plan to get there.

Not only that, but the strategy will allow you to define how you will measure your successes along the way. As the saying goes, 'What gets measured, gets done.' So, having clear business outcomes articulated will help to keep everyone focused on what needs to happen and by when.

A strategy will set you up for clarity and success. It's as simple as that. People will have clear goals, objectives and measurements of success. Without this strategy step in place, you may as well put a blindfold on every individual in the organisation, place them all at the entrance of a crazy maze and wish them luck. A spine-chilling thought.

Let me take you back to the story of Tracy, the People Director from earlier in the chapter.

So, what happened next for her?

Well, she did get the board back together after the grievance was resolved. They held some quite challenging, soul-searching sessions to articulate what 'leading a coaching culture' meant.

They reviewed their vision, purpose and what a high-performing organisation with a coaching culture meant to them. They peeled back layer upon layer to get under the skin of what it meant in a deep way to them. They identified which behaviours were and were not acceptable, how they were going to live and breathe the culture and what they were going to do if they or others were going off track. The sessions weren't plain-sailing and there were difficult moments throughout as each board member took the time to reflect on the way forward.

Nonetheless, they experienced several breakthrough moments that allowed them to revise the original strategy that was in place with greater thought and clarity. This time round, it felt like they were bringing together the cultural expectations and the business strategy, not operating them as two separate entities.

They were by no means back to square one, but they'd taken one step back to go many strides forward. That's OK. That's cultural change for you.

ONE HAND TIED BEHIND YOUR BACK

If you don't have a strategy in place to ensure that you know how you're going to build and shape a coaching culture, you won't have the time, space or resources for coaching conversations to take place. Furthermore, without a clear strategy in place, nobody will be clear on why a coaching culture is necessary, what it really means and how it will all come to life. The focus and energy will just not be there.

Let's break them down.

1.   No time and space

Cultural change takes time and effort. It doesn't happen overnight or at the wave of a magic wand. In any organisation, strategic plans need to be given the time and space to make the vision a reality, and the plan to come to fruition. Without the right amount of time and space to build a coaching culture, it just won't happen. It won't be a strategic priority, and this will give enough people all the excuses they need not to make a change. This will no doubt leave you feeling more frustrated than ever as one dose of the 'yerbuts' quickly takes hold and spreads like a pandemic throughout the organisation.

2.   No resources

As highlighted earlier, it's the culture of the organisation that will determine whether the business strategy is achieved. When it's that important, which it absolutely is, it will require the right resources putting in place, and that will include people, systems and technology. If you can't invest in the right areas with the right people focused on the right things, you'll probably end up feeling like you've got one hand tied behind your back. In the very worst cases, it will be both hands tied with heavy-duty rope. Working like that is certainly not going to help you to build a coaching culture any time soon.

CASE STUDY: SILVA HOMES

Back in late 2019, an email came into the office. It was from Rob, the then People, Digital and Change Director from Silva Homes, a medium-sized Housing Association based in Bracknell. They were going through significant transformation. In fact, when I say 'significant', it was HUGE. A major restructure in the business had resulted in approximately 50% new people being recruited, which created both opportunity and challenge in equal measures. I later found out that building a coaching culture was the new aspirational cultural goal. So, I was delighted to hear that, thanks to a quick Google search, the services and solutions of Coaching Culture sprang up. Not bad considering we hadn't even focused on SEO marketing at that time.

It soon became clear that Silva Homes wanted to find a coaching partner to support their managers through the continuing change. The reassuring thing for us was that the CEO and the People, Digital and Change Director knew that a simple coaching programme would only go part way towards helping people lead and coach through change. They also knew that they had to have a longer-term strategy in place to build capability, as well as building a coaching culture.

And that's where Coaching Culture came in.

It was March 2020 and the threat of Covid 19 was rising by the day. I set off on the three-hour journey to Bracknell to have a meeting with the Director. We knew that we needed to fully understand the organisational situation, so that the most suitable strategy could be defined and the right solutions implemented.

It's a day that will be lodged in my memory forever.

I remember stopping at the services on the way to grab a coffee and realised that the usually busy roads were eerily quiet. The service station that was ordinarily hustling and bustling with people travelling around the country was like a ghost town. I even remember commenting to the lady who served my coffee… it felt like the rest of the world knew something that we didn't.

It was the very start of the global pandemic.

I arrived at the office in Bracknell and sat down with the Director. I was armed with a host of carefully planned coaching questions to help me to understand what the current situation was and where the organisation aimed to be in the future. Any strategy that was to be put in place had to be fully aligned with the organisational values and any people policies that were already in place.

Having seen many a change programme fail, and having a framework for success, I was happy to be able to bring years of experience, fresh perspectives and guidance to the meeting. The purpose was to really get clear on what the first three years could look like as they embarked upon their change journey.

As we worked together over the coming months, and as the challenges of remote working took over our daily lives, the strategy soon started to take shape. We presented to the board and the senior leadership team, and they bought in to the focus on culture and how coaching could help their teams through change. But it wasn't just about organisational change anymore; it was now about navigating an unprecedented change that had never been experienced before. Why? Because the strategy swiftly needed to include the challenges faced by remote working, and how coaching conversations would help.

Thankfully, the strategy was heavily supported by the CEO, and the fact that he had experienced the benefits of coaching first hand. He'd had several sessions with an Executive Coach that had really highlighted to him the difference that effective coaching conversations could make. And while the pandemic could have wobbled the strategic direction, it did the opposite. It accelerated the need to feel the benefits of a coaching culture.

To get sign off for the strategy and the budget, that placed coaching conversations firmly at the heart of the business, felt fabulous. It was energising to know we would be partnering with such a forward-thinking organisation that recognised the importance of their people and the power of coaching conversations. Not only that, but the whole strategy was also being championed at the very top from the start.

Fast forward three years to November 2022.

We invited Rob (the People, Digital and Change Director) to do a fireside-style interview on stage at the Coaching Culture conference in Nottingham. He showcased the work that had been achieved over the three years... here's a snippet of what he said:

"Working with Jo and the team at Coaching Culture has been fantastic... We've been identified by Best Companies as a housing association to watch and we've had one of our highest engagement scores. I'm absolutely sure that the coaching and cultural work has been a really important part, as we've seen an improvement in the quality of conversations. Not only that, but I also see a much more engaged leadership team. One of the biggest things has been changing people's mindset. While we're still on that journey, we're in a much stronger place than we were before..."

Rob Smyth, former People, Digital and Change Director, Silva Homes

WHAT TO DO

Step 1: Define the organisational values and culture codes

As culture is about everyday behaviours and norms, it's important that any strategy focused on building a coaching culture starts there. Most organisations like to define their values and then the associated culture codes to articulate the guiding principles of behaviour. These must mean something to employees, customers and other stakeholders.

It's clear from the organisations that we work with that the most successful ones are those that co-create them with the people who work there. When done well, the process allows people to have a voice, share what really matters to them, and gets their buy in along the way. Much better than having a big reveal with an unexpected 'da daaaaa' moment at the annual conference.

A good place to start is facilitating the board's identification of the values and behaviours that matter most and, just as importantly, which ones don't. It's important to keep focused on how they will help to achieve a coaching culture and the overall strategic plan. It's important at this stage not to limit the possibilities and to capture as many ideas as possible. It's likely there will be themes arising among a very long list of values. Bundling them up into smaller, more meaningful groups will allow them to be taken out to the rest of the organisation for further input and feedback.

As more and more teams openly share their thoughts and ideas in workshops, a picture about what employees value and don't value will start to emerge. Once finalised and agreed upon, many organisations will then announce the values, stick the words on the wall and assume it's a fait accompli. That's where they go wrong. The most important part of any work that is done to articulate principles of behaviours and norms is to make sure they are lived and breathed and become part of everyday language; they need to be articulated as culture codes. These are words and phrases that are both memorable and meaningful to everyone in the organisation. Think quirky sayings and idioms, rather than a handful of words stuck on a wall.

Step 2: Create the cultural roadmap

Building on the evidence that was presented to the board proving the need for a coaching culture, it's time to define the three-to-five-year strategic goals. It's essential to have a medium to long term horizon because, believe me, culture doesn't change overnight. Consider the evidence and look at the areas that will have the greatest impact, while answering the all-important question: what are the big rocks that will move the cultural dial?

The strategic roadmap with a three-to-five-year lens is just that. A roadmap. It certainly shouldn't be set in stone. It needs to be a clearly defined plan with goals and objectives to achieve along the way, yet it should also have enough flexibility to change as new information arises over time.

Strategy work to develop and embed a coaching culture will include areas such as values and culture codes, everyday norms, coaching environments, communication and engagement, coaching capability, feedback mechanisms, coaching policies and expectations, use of technology, and how to reward and celebrate coaching successes. All areas of the employee life cycle must be considered, as coaching conversations will undoubtedly impact upon them all.

In addition, it's important to agree what the measures of success will be for each stage of the strategic plan. We all know that some are easier to measure than others. The most common measures include, recruitment, employee engagement surveys, pulse surveys, talent retention, diversity and inclusion, the number of internal promotions and the number and quality of management conversations.

While the thinking behind this plan may start with the People team, the entire organisation will create the culture. It goes without saying therefore that the coaching culture strategy needs to be an integral part of the overall business strategy that measures all key business metrics.

Step 3: Provide the time, space and resource for coaching

So, you have a vision for a coaching culture, the board are bought in, the values are clear, and the strategy is coming together nicely. It's now time to ensure the cultural aspiration is given the right time, space, and resources to come to fruition. We work with many different organisations who have different budget levels to invest in a coaching culture. Nonetheless, there is a strong commonality that stands out: those who are most committed to building a coaching culture find a way. In fact, it's becoming increasingly common for coaching to have its own line on the organisational P&L because it's seen as that important.

However, if budgets are tight, rather than give up at the first hurdle, more organisations think creatively. That could include using budgets from a variety of business units or functions. In other words, it doesn't just come down to the People team to fund it, which makes perfect sense when culture is everyone's responsibility. Not only that, but in a coaching culture, everyone benefits.

As resources includes people too, it's important to look at the roles that may be needed to support this cultural movement. While some organisations may have a 'Director of People and Culture', others may have a 'Head of Coaching'. It's certainly symbolic of the strategic intent and sends out a clear message when you have someone with the word 'culture' or 'coaching' in their title. It doesn't stop there though. Coaching culture champions should also be identified to beat the drum. Most importantly, while all the board must be able to role-model a coaching culture, the board will still need a clear sponsor and champion of the cultural change programme. The person responsible for keeping the strategy on track and holding the board to account when making decisions and progress will be a key component of your success.

Furthermore, the strategy must allow for time and space for people to build a coaching culture. This will include time to win hearts and minds, to learn how to coach, to be coached, to adopt new ways of working and technology. No stone should be left unturned when considering cultural and behavioural change. To truly embed this as a new way of communicating in the organisation, people must feel fully supported to go on the journey. Some organisations have even started to introduce coaching policies and guidelines to ensure the new way of working is adopted.

EXERCISE: PLAN THE JOURNEY

Even though the nuts and bolts of the coaching culture strategy tend to be developed by the People team, it needs to be owned and championed by the entire board. Committing the strategy to paper, with goals, objectives, milestones, resources and measures, will ensure your cultural aspirations have every chance of being achieved.

Having a clear 'from' and 'to' position helps to articulate what needs to happen along the way and, like any strategy, the following key questions need to be answered:

- Where are you now?

- Where do you want to be?

- How will you get there?

This exercise is made up of a series of coaching questions focused to help build the strategic plan. It's best done as a collaborative workshop with the business leaders who are responsible for the cultural strategy.

Step 1: Where are you now?

1. What are the stated values and culture codes?

2. What are the accepted norms?

3. What are the accepted codes of behaviour?

4. What is the current coaching capability like?

5. How do coaching conversations take place?

6. What time and space is given for coaching?

7. What time and space is given for self-reflection?

8. What resources are provided to ensure better conversations?

9. What is the current coaching capability like?

10. How are coaching outcomes rewarded?

11. How is feedback shared and captured?

12. What are the expectations around coaching conversations?

13. What technology is in place to support coaching?

14. How are conversations measured?

15. How are coaching successes celebrated?

Step 2: Where do you want to be?

With a future view on the same questions, answer one by one, 'where do you want to be?' This should be as visionary and as creative as you dare to dream.

Step 3: How will you get there?

Finally, the all-important question of 'how are you going to get there?' needs to be answered. Furthermore, it's important to cover off and address any areas that may be getting in the way of success too. Creating a simple one-page strategy document will help keep you focused and on track. As change isn't a linear process, some organisations start at step one of the seven step framework and work through the steps over time. Other organisations we work with tend to start small, with a pilot group, then expand over time. This may mean starting at step four or five of the framework, then going back to step one when they have success stories to share. They simply prefer to create a buzz of excitement that ripples around the organisation. Rather than being a strategy that is pushed onto others, it becomes a strategy that is willingly pulled from within.

For example, depending on what works best for your organisation, you may choose to run a focused and blended pilot programme that focuses on building a coaching culture. Feedback can then be gathered, and all learnings can then inform future changes. Some organisations start with certain groups of people, often the leadership teams.

It's important to recognise that cultural change can take a long time, depending on the size of your organisation. Capturing the green shoots of change and cultural successes along the way is important to stay focused and motivated to achieve the ultimate vision. Constant reminders through company communications, internal marketing campaigns, team meetings and in one-to-ones will help to embed and sustain cultural changes.

HEAD TO JOWRIGHT.COM
TO DOWNLOAD MORE RESOURCES

TOP TEN TAKEAWAYS

In this chapter, we have learned:

1. To align the coaching cultural strategy to the overall business strategy.

2. The culture will determine whether the business strategy is achieved.

3. To align the senior leaders with the cultural strategy.

4. To ensure the senior leaders can articulate and demonstrate what is expected.

5. The board must provide time, space and resources for coaching.

6. To co-create the organisational values and behaviours.

7. To create culture codes to articulate principles of behaviour in a meaningful and measurable way.

8. To create a coaching culture roadmap with clear milestones and measures of success.

9. To create a coaching budget line on the organisational P&L.

10. To ensure the right roles are put in place to support the cultural ambitions.

CHAPTER 7

ENGAGE

Win hearts and minds

"

Convince people
and you win their
minds. Inspire
people and you
win their hearts.

"

ROB KAUFMAN

NEITHER FULLY DEAD NOR FULLY ALIVE

Have you ever looked around your organisation and seen people tearing around with their backsides on fire, but not really understanding where they're heading? Or worse still, they're walking around like zombies, neither fully dead nor fully alive, as they're just going through the motions until something better comes along.

Probably sounds all too familiar, right?

It's very similar to when people are part of a strategic change programme – one that has been conjured up behind the closed doors of the board room. You know the ones, with dark wood panelling and plush leather seats, or the newer versions, shrouded in frosted glass, like a goldfish bowl filled with murky water, where you know something is going on inside, but you're never quite sure what.

When the powers-that-be have decided the strategy, a clear way forward, they then hastily communicate it so you can all dive straight into the implementation stage. This misses out one of the most important pieces of the jigsaw: the stage where communication moves from one-way to two-way and everyone impacted is engaged, their opinions are heard and hearts and minds are not only won but people are left itching to take the next step.

What tends to happen instead is that the reason behind the new way forward isn't fully explained. Instead, the first people get wind of it is when an email pops into their already full inbox, or worse still, it's a calendar invitation for a training course that they have zero interest in attending. If you think that sounds ridiculous, let me assure you that it's not. It's happening all too often.

From my experience, change programmes fail when communication is just one-way. People don't just change when they're told to change. How simple (and boring) would life be if that was the case?

Imagine the scenario…

Your CEO is stood in front of the whole organisation. 'Hey everybody! We've decided it's time to make some changes…' And everybody cheers and claps loudly, just itching to be part of the mystery changes.

It just doesn't happen like that, and that's completely understandable too.

Why? Because we're human.

As humans, we have an innate desire to feel a sense of belonging, a deeper connection to a higher purpose. Or at the very least, we want to know what the hell is going on and how it impacts us. This leads me onto a cringeworthy phrase that I've heard a lot throughout my career. And I'm sure you have too…

'It wasn't my decision…' Pause. 'It was my boss's.'

It's a phrase that sends the hairs on the back of my neck sticking upright and certainly not the sort of thing you want to hear from anyone in a leadership or management position. Nonetheless, it's an all-too-common display of zero accountability, because they didn't buy in to the decision earlier on.

And we wonder why, according to Harvard Business Review, over 70% of cultural change programmes fail.

It's because, when changes are enforced and people are simply told what to do, it's human nature to push back. Our inner rebel screams out, 'I don't think so…'

Let's face it, there's not many of us who like being told what to do. It reminds us too much of being children again. Just think about the hoo-ha that face masks caused during a global pandemic. OK, let's not go there.

Now that we're adults, we like to share our opinions, feel listened to, and collaborated with. It helps us to feel valued. On that note, I'm going to contradict myself here.

There are certain times when we do like to be simply told what to do. When we don't want to be asked for our opinions, to have our hearts and minds won, or to feel collaborated with. That is during extreme events, like if we find ourselves in a burning building or being chased by a sabre-tooth tiger. Just point us in the right direction and we'll run like hell.

But apart from those rare occasions, make engaging your teams a priority. P-LEASE!

COMMUNICATE, COMMUNICATE AND COMMUNICATE SOME MORE

So, meanwhile, back in the boardroom…

The strategy has been carefully planned out, there's a clear path to achieve the organisational cultural and business goals. It's now time to not only communicate the plan but to win hearts and minds and engage the troops.

I heard a lovely quote the other day from the founder of Connect Three, Colin Lamb:

"If you think you've communicated enough, multiply it by ten, and you might get near, then multiply it by ten again, then keep communicating."

In fact, according to research, it takes the average person hearing a message at least seven times to truly get it, understand it and act upon it.

The point is this: you simply cannot over-communicate.

However, don't be fooled that sending seven emails ticks the box. Effective communication must be a blend of all types: formal, informal, one-way, two-way, written, verbal, face-to-face, virtual, meetings, one-to-one conversations, conferences, workshops, video, corridor conversations and many more…

While variety and repetition matter, winning hearts and minds for people to think, feel and act differently must be the goal.

The ENGAGE step of the seven steps to building a coaching culture framework includes focusing on communication and hearts and minds. It's not acceptable to fail to communicate multiple times. And when I say communicate, that's not just one-way traffic. That's having a clear communication and engagement strategy in place to continue to get support for the cultural changes, and to set up internal networks to ensure voices and opinions are heard.

Most organisations do this in the form of 'change champions', those people who are excited to be the ambassadors of the intended change. It's also important for organisations to identify a member of the board to be the sponsor of the change, the one who leads the programme from the top, the one who holds the organisation to account every step of the way.

If you think an external speaker will help to endorse the message, then engage an expert to inspire the masses.

It's certainly not the step of the process where an email or two are simply popped into the inbox!

WHAT'S IN IT FOR ME?

It's one of the most important steps of the process, and one that can often be overlooked or done without real purpose and meaning. This is the stage when the awareness starts to build, people become interested and intrigued about what the change will mean to them. They will start to ask the all-important W.I.I.F.M. question (what's in it for me?), and quite rightly so. It's important at this stage that the benefits of building a coaching culture are laid out, coaching is demystified, and momentum starts to build.

Get this right and you will be the hero or heroine of the cultural change programme, the one wearing the cape with a giant S on the back. As progress is made, testimonials will start to flood in and, most importantly, behaviours will start to change for the better.

The time invested in this step is key to the successful embedding of a culture. You are starting to stir up interest in others that will leave them feeling like they have an important part to play in the cultural fortunes of the organisation.

At this stage, this is no longer just a good idea nestled in the safety of the board room. By now, the cat has been let out of the bag, the secret is shared and you're on your way to making a change! And to avoid the 'Head of Scaremongering' or the 'Chair of the Juicy Gossip committee' stepping in at every stage, your role is to ensure the communications and engagement plan is executed brilliantly.

This step is where you and your change champions bring out your soap boxes and shout from the rooftops about how a coaching culture is the way to make the organisation great. Share the many benefits, share case studies that are steeped in successful real-life stories, and without a shadow of a doubt, you must answer these three important questions:

WHY? – Explain why the organisation is moving in this direction.

WHAT? – Explain what the change will be and what it will mean for teams and individuals.

HOW? – Explain how you envisage getting there together.

Remember, this is about enabling the organisation to **think** that there is another way so they can **feel** excited and inspired to **do** something about it. This will mean that they'll have the confidence and capability to enact change.

This is when the beating heart of the organisation starts to beat a little bit faster, excited by the art of the possible, and you have a very important part to play in making that happen.

AVOIDING A YERBUT PANDEMIC

If you don't engage those impacted and instead choose to leap headfirst into the next step of the process, you will be met by utter confusion. The army of change-resisters will come out in force. Your desire to build coaching capabilities and change behaviours for the long term won't happen. Instead, you'll be peppered with unanswered questions, mutterings behind closed doors, and before you know it, the invitations for the organisational pity-parties will start being sent out to every person in the business. The inner rebels will be shouting 'we don't think so' from every rooftop.

One dose of the yerbuts will soon develop into an organisational pandemic, all because you haven't won the hearts and minds of your people.

Now don't get me wrong, some people will not only happily fall into line, but they'll also be excited by new opportunities. They're the positive go-getters who embrace change without question. They trust the leaders to have done the strategic thinking and trust they are making the right decisions. They are the ones who you want to grab hold of the opportunity to be ambassadors of change, to partner up with the rebels, to sprinkle their positivity and motivation amongst their colleagues and spread the word. They will spread the message and beat the drum to inspire others. They will be an invaluable part of the cultural movement.

Put simply, they are pure gold.

CASE STUDY: GOVERNMENT AGENCY

One of our customers is a government agency. They are very clear about their strategy to build a coaching culture. They had been implementing several solutions to embed coaching conversations into their culture for a few years. They were out of the starting blocks and on their way to success. They had an external coach coaching senior leaders, they offered a coaching capability programme to several employees, and the whole organisation had access to our library of digital coaching content. They were certainly serious about the impact that coaching made. Furthermore, they were one of a growing number of organisations leading the way with an internal coaching and mentoring community.

The coaching and mentoring community had been set up in 2020 to not only embrace the cultural strategy but to champion coaching and mentoring in the organisation. To build a community of true coaching and mentoring fans could have been considered an ambitious goal at that time because, if you remember back, we were in the throes of navigating our way through a global pandemic. Nonetheless, those organisations who were truly listening to their employees ensured that coaching and mentoring became the go-to support system during such a challenging time.

The community was set up and officially launched. Nonetheless, it became apparent over time, with the fresh challenges posed by hybrid working, that they weren't getting together as much as they liked, so they weren't fully bonding as a true community. For some, the busyness of the day job was simply getting in the way. This meant that all the hard work that was being invested into building a coaching culture was not being fully championed by the very people who had been given the internal drum to beat.

The team who was responsible for leading the community knew that more had to be done to bring the community together, remind them of their purpose and their journey and showcase their growing number of achievements. To achieve this, they organised a gathering for the community members to reconnect.

A couple of the team members had seen me speak at a conference and saw with their own eyes my passion for this topic. To be fair, I can get a bit excitable when talking about the importance of a coaching culture and all the benefits that it brings. Because of this, they invited me along to talk to the group, with the hope of inspiring them, reigniting their passion, and sharing the important message that everybody is responsible for changing the culture. I was thrilled to accept and, in no time at all, I was heading over to beautiful Yorkshire.

As a Lancashire girl, I always loved to drive across the Pennines to the county of Yorkshire. It was where I'd lived for many years post-university, so it held a special place in my heart. On this day in January 2023, it was especially beautiful. It was the day I was due to talk to the coaching and mentoring group. I looked up and there wasn't a cloud in the sky. I quietly smiled to myself as the sun shone down and I prepared myself to beat the coaching and mentoring drum.

For 45 minutes, I spoke and engaged the group. I reminded them that what they were doing wasn't just changing the culture; it was changing lives. They were building confidence, resilience and supporting others to believe in themselves. While others were benefiting because they were giving up their time and focus to coach and mentor them, this community of positive and passionate individuals were developing too. Yet another example of a win-win.

I wanted to leave the group with something to think about. So, I left them with three coaching questions to mull over:

What do you want your legacy to be as a group?

What more could you do to engage the organisation in coaching?

What one action will you commit to doing from today?

The feedback was tremendous.

"Jo's session really hit the mark and generated so many ideas on how we can build that culture of coaching. Feeling the energy and enthusiasm from the group, and hearing their suggestions, we just know we've created an army of coaching and mentoring supporters!"

Joanne Scott, Learning and Organisational Development Project Lead

WHAT TO DO

Step 1: Define the communications and engagement plan

This is one of the most important steps in any change journey. Building a coaching culture is no different. Most organisations communicate, but they don't necessarily engage. What do I mean by that? They focus on delivering one-way messages providing minimal opportunity for people to reflect, ask questions, or clarify understanding. The magic happens when people are fully engaged and have bought in. One-way communication could include conferences, webinars, emails, and intranet announcements. Whereas good engagement includes reflection, discussion, and action planning. This could be in the form of workshops, team meetings, one-to-one meetings. The plan must define the audience, the purpose of the communication and the key messages, whilst including as many modes of communication as possible. It's important to remember that what works for one person won't be the same for another. If the message is clear, concise and consistent, whilst remembering to be suited to those receiving the message, then the more types of communication, the better.

Workshops are particularly powerful when engaging large groups. They're a great way to start to hand the baton of change over to the people who will make the change happen.

This might mean asking coaching questions such as:

- What are your reflections?

- What do you like about the changes?

- What does this change mean to you?

- What obstacles do you foresee, if any?

- How will you overcome any obstacles?

- What do you need to do differently?

- What support do you need to make it happen?

It's important to note that the communication and engagement strategy must be a dynamic document that is lived and breathed. Not something that gets done once, put in a drawer, and forgotten about. Progress must be measured, feedback captured and plans adapted accordingly.

Step 2: Recruit an army of coaching champions

Any change initiative needs its flag-bearers, those positive go-getters who really embrace change and are happy to influence their colleagues around them. Their positivity is infectious. They inspire others with their can-do attitude. They can light up any room. They are the stark opposite of the mood-hoovers, who sap the living daylights out of anyone who dares to step in their way.

Most organisations we work with ask people to raise their hand and nominate themselves to be a coaching champion. It's important to go where the energy is. It will make your role easier and more rewarding as you embark on this cultural change journey. It then becomes the job of the coaching champions to help spread the good word.

To volunteer to be a coaching champion, they are likely to ask:

- What will be the impact on me?

- How much time will it take?

- Will it add extra work to my usual role?

- What exactly does it entail?

- What development will I receive?

- What exposure to key stakeholders will I receive?

- What will be the benefits?

- Who can I contact for support?

It's not just about the recruitment of this great group of people though. It's important to plan how you will engage and develop them too.

It's important to consider:

- Why are they doing this?

- How will you keep them engaged too?

- How will you develop them?

- How will you engage their line managers?

- How will you keep them connected to the overall strategic goals?

They are an important piece in the cultural change jigsaw puzzle. They are there to infiltrate the organisation, to role-model coaching and share successes at every opportunity. A coaching ninja in every sense of the word.

Step 3: Shout from the rooftops

So, the communication and engagement strategy has been created, the coaching champions have been recruited and it's time to execute the plan. It's time to shout from the rooftops about the direction of travel. The purpose of this stage is to excite and inspire, demystify coaching, share what it is and isn't, share the proposed plans, and gather momentum about the power and benefit of coaching conversations.

It's important to note that communication and engagement isn't a one-time event. It needs to be constant and consistent – a regular drum beat of information, updates, inspirational stories and news to focus the mind. It's a great time to create a buzz of activity and intrigue. The more positive messages that are shared, the more people will start to become interested and engaged in what's happening. It moves from a push to a pull strategy when people are keen to find out more and take part in the cultural changes.

For some organisations, this stage is about winning hearts and minds about the vision and changes that will take place over time. It's the time to give opportunities for two-way communication and engagement, sharing evidence and case studies from other organisations. For those who have chosen to take the 'start small, then expand over time' approach, they are likely to already have several internal case studies and positive stories to share.

No matter which strategic course of action is taken, as more and more people start to see, hear, and feel the benefits, others will start to stand up and listen. Imagine a group of inquisitive meerkats. It's like that. And when the fear of missing out (f.o.m.o.) starts to kick in, you know you're onto a winner.

EXERCISE: PLAN TO WIN HEARTS AND MINDS

The purpose of this exercise is to help you to shape your communication and engagement strategy. In some organisations, the communication and engagement strategies are the responsibility of a specialist team in the business. In others, it's the role of the People team who are often the driving force behind the cultural changes. This is best done as a workshop between a small number of key stakeholders.

Communication and engagement strategy workshop

1. Choose the right people to be in the room

This is likely to include representatives from the People and Communications team as well as the board sponsor for building a coaching culture.

2. Answer the following questions as a group:

- Who is the audience?

- What is the purpose of the message?

- What do you want people to think afterwards?

- What do you want people to feel afterwards?

- What do you want people to do differently afterwards?

- What are the key messages?

- What modes of communication will be utilised and when?

- Who will do this?

- What are the measures of success?

- How will progress be measured?

- How will feedback be captured?

3. Create a communications and engagement plan on a page

This should include headlines, including: purpose, audience, key messages, modes of communication (by who, by when), and measures of success.

HEAD TO JOWRIGHT.COM
TO DOWNLOAD MORE RESOURCES

TOP TEN TAKEAWAYS

In this chapter, we have learned:

1. The importance of communication – communicate, communicate and communicate some more!

2. To use a variety of communication types delivered in different ways.

3. To create a clear, concise and consistent communication and engagement strategy.

4. To win hearts and minds so people think, feel and act differently.

5. To provide the time and space for two-way engagement and reflection.

6. To share the many benefits of a coaching culture.

7. To share as many positive and inspirational coaching stories as possible.

8. To demystify coaching by sharing what it is and what it isn't.

9. To build a network of coaching champions.

10. To keep beating the drum to reinforce the messages of cultural change.

CHAPTER 8

GROW

Grow coaching capability

"

We are what
we repeatedly do.
Excellence then,
is not an act,
but a habit.

"

ARISTOTLE

HOW NOT TO APPROACH A COACHING CONVERSATION

'**S**o, Jo...' my boss said, in an irritatingly soothing voice… 'How do you think that meeting went?'

Uh-oh!

He must be asking me because he thinks it was awful, is what I instantly thought.

Worse still was that he stayed silent for what seemed like a lifetime until I rummaged around in my mind to find the right words.

Personally, I thought the meeting had gone well. It was a sales meeting, we were presenting our product range to a potential customer, who acted more like a market trader than a Senior Procurement Manager for a large, branded restaurant chain. He was confident, brash, and desperate to screw us down to the lowest price.

I'd done my prep, asked some pretty good questions and listened intently to what was being said. I'd then presented our solutions, carefully repeating back the same words that the potential customer used.

We'd come away with some clear next steps to review the pricing. He'd seemed visibly shocked at the numbers. As I was new to sales, his reaction unnerved me. Nonetheless, I later learned to love this all-too-common reaction. The one when the buyer shakes their head in utter dismay, sucks their cheeks in and lets out a well-rehearsed whistling noise. It eventually became part of the fun of the sales game for me. The sharper the intake of breath, the more fun I had.

Nonetheless, on that day, it just fed my inner imposter, which was having an absolute field day.

'Err… I think it was OK,' was the best I could muster.

'What would you do differently next time?' His brow was furrowed, and he had a concerned expression on his face.

This was getting serious.

Maybe I didn't ask the right questions, didn't spot the obvious buying signals, laughed at the wrong moments.

I desperately tried to think what I could have done differently. My mind went blank. I gave him a quick answer to try to appease him and get myself out of this increasingly awkward situation. Bear in mind that we still hadn't even made it to the car!

His expression softened.

'I thought it went really well, Jo,' he said with a smile on his face. 'We achieved the objective of the meeting, and we now have the opportunity to present another proposal with a wider range than we thought.'

Whatttt???

Relief flooded over me.

Why didn't he just say that in the first place? I thought. It would have stopped the massive discomfort I'd been feeling in the five minutes since the meeting.

Unbeknown to me, my boss was in 'post-meeting coach-mode.' Fresh off a leadership development course, he had decided to practice his newfound techniques on me. Rather than gently signposting me to his new way of communicating, he just did it. Not only did it take me by surprise, but it jet-propelled my inner imposter into the stratosphere.

He'd excelled in 'how not to approach a coaching conversation'!

PUT PEOPLE FIRST, AND THE RESULTS WILL FOLLOW

It would be impossible to change the culture into one where managers are having more meaningful and effective conversations without growing coaching capability along the way. And when I say 'capability', I mean changing the way people think and feel, which will change the way they act. Developing both mindset and skillset and busting a few die-hard coaching myths along the way is the best option for growing capability.

In fact, why stop at managers? Everyone should have the capability to coach because it's a way of 'being'. Put simply, it's a life skill. Not just an approach to be used in the workplace, it's an impactful way of communicating in everyday life. Believe me, it encourages curiosity, develops relationships, builds trust and, at work, it directly impacts the bottom line.

To quote Caspar Craven, the author of *Be More Human*: 'Put people first, and the results will follow.'

Coaching conversations enable people to do just that.

The **GROW** step of this framework focuses on growing coaching capability. Now some organisations will dive straight into this step, to give coaching a go, then when they see the signs that capability is growing and spot the green shoots of change emerging, they gather the evidence and head straight back to step one to go all in on cultural change. There is no right or wrong answer. As I've already said, change isn't a linear process, and each organisational strategy will be different. It's what works best for you and your organisation. Let's face it, it's also how open to building a coaching culture your board are.

If you've already won hearts and minds, and you have got people excited about building a coaching culture, then by this stage you should have people lining up to develop their coaching skills. If you haven't, then you may find that the coaching sceptics will drag their feet like sulky teenagers onto any development solutions that you put in place.

WHEN THE MAGIC HAPPENS

Growing coaching capability is crucial. If there was one quote that sums it up beautifully, it would be this one by Sir Richard Branson:

'Train people well enough so that they can leave.

Treat them well enough so they don't want to...'

In fact, I'd go one step further and say:

'Train people well enough so that they can leave.

Coach them well enough so they don't want to...'

Coaching is another level of capability that moves way beyond 'training'. It's a mindset, a way of being. When people are asked questions, listened to, valued, empowered and trusted to do their job, let's face it, they won't want to leave.

When the war for talent is real, keeping and developing your people is a vital step towards organisational success.

When I talk about coaching capability, I'm not talking 'expert' level. Different people will need different levels of capability. Some people will want to have formal accreditations, whereas others will need an introduction to coaching to give them the confidence to just give it a go.

You'll often hear me comparing coaching capability to cooking! What do I mean by this? Well, we should all know how to cook, but we don't all need to know how to be a Michelin star chef.

Well, it's the same for coaching!

We should all know how to have a coaching conversation, but we don't all need to be professionally accredited coaches. And that's why there are many different levels:

1. Self-coaching

2. Peer-to-peer coaching conversations

3. Managers adopting a coaching style

4. Internally accredited coaches

5. Externally accredited team coaches

6. Externally accredited executive coaches

The magic truly happens on a large scale when managers can have effective and regular conversations with their teams and colleagues. They can set clear goals, give and receive feedback and create accountability in others. It can feel even more magical when colleagues are encouraged to help and coach each other too.

'Resulting in what?' you may be asking.

The answer is: 'Greater trust and higher performance.' And who doesn't want that?

Growing coaching capability must be a 'given' now in all organisations that want to be fit for both the needs of current employees as well as those of the future. Too much has changed in the world of work to ignore how people have changed their expectations of what they want from their managers.

The command and control, 'tell' style that dominated in the past is now considered old school. In fact, I'd go one step further and say that it is 'totally out of date'. Employees have much higher expectations these days, and quite rightly so. In addition, the pandemic has only accelerated a trend that was already happening. People want their managers to listen, to empathise, to care, to trust, to include, to show an interest in their wellbeing, to develop them, to allow them to grow and flourish, to see beyond the bottom line.

The best managers recognise that, by caring for their people and trusting them, there is a direct correlation with the bottom line, creating a successful and growing business. A win-win all round.

It's your role as a leader to assess the level of coaching capability in the business, and then provide the solutions that will build and hone the organisational coaching muscle that changes behaviours for the long term.

THE CONSEQUENCE OF SH*T MANAGERS

The consequence of sh*t managers is a costly business. All the time and effort that goes into recruiting top talent, only to have confidence crushed and stress levels raised by managers who do not know how to communicate effectively is devastating.

From my experience, when asked whether they coach their teams, most managers will say 'yes'. What that really means is that they take the time to ask their team questions, then without much of a thought, they dive straight in with their own ideas and solutions. Giving the team a 'get out of jail free' card for not even having to think for themselves. At the same time, the manager feeds their own ego because they've answered their own question. Nobody learns. Nobody develops. It's such a lose-lose situation.

In today's world, more and more people seem to feel the need to be 'on' 24/7, with notifications pinging from every device and distractions-a-plenty. As a result, the art of deep listening seems to be in short supply. In Stephen Covey's *The 7 Habits of Highly Effective People*, he calls it 'empathic listening'; the type that listens to understand, not to be understood. After all, an effective coaching conversation is about asking powerful questions and listening to understand.

It's becoming an increasingly popular viewpoint that to have no level of coaching capability is simply not acceptable for managers today. In fact, I'd go as far as saying no-one should have the privilege of being a manager of people without some level of coaching capability. It's that important. It should be the accepted rite of passage.

Unfortunately, what happens all too often is that people are promoted into management levels through showing exceptional technical capabilities, rather than people skills. Could you imagine giving someone the keys to your car without them having passed their driving test? It just wouldn't happen. Having some level of coaching capability if you're a people manager should be seen in the same light.

And when managers don't have the capability to coach their own teams, what can they do? They send their people to be coached by a member of the People team – in other words, they are expecting their colleagues to do their work for them! This leaves the already over-stretched People function feeling even more busy, at a time when enabling managers should be a higher priority.

Sounds all too familiar, right?

CASE STUDY: KAINOS GROUP PLC

Kainos is a leading technology company that provides information technology services, consulting, and software solutions all around the world. They are true experts in digital transformation. It makes me beam with pride to say that they have been a loyal customer of Coaching Culture's since 2019.

When Emma Lidgett joined as the Head of Talent, Development and Learning back in 2019, the organisation was growing rapidly, and it was clear that people needed more development. Managers were having conversations, just not coaching-style conversations. They weren't flexing their styles. One size was trying to fit all. This was driving a more directive-focused style of conversation, reduced autonomy and not supporting the development conversations they wanted. And let's face it, that's not the most conducive environment in which people thrive.

Thankfully, it was obvious to Emma that managers needed to be able to have more effective conversations. She asked herself the question: 'How best can we support our people?'

The answer was glaringly obvious.

'We need to build a coaching culture.'

Despite having an Effective Manager programme already in place that focused on the fundamentals of management, such as how to have one-to-ones, and how to give feedback, there was a need for managers to be able to adopt a coaching style.

As the organisation was rapidly growing around the world, a blended solution of digital and face-to-face was needed for smarter scaling.

Fortunately, Emma did have the autonomy and a blank piece of paper to do what was needed. So, armed with ideas and a shopping list, she headed off to the annual World of Learning exhibition, on the hunt for the most effective solutions to help the management capability challenge.

This is where she met the team at Coaching Culture for the first time.

Three things stood out to Emma at the time:

1. The digital solutions offered a wide range of relevant content that complemented the Effective Manager programme.

2. The team at Coaching Culture had a huge passion for the difference coaching conversations make.

3. Coaching Culture shared the same values as Kainos and were therefore the right organisation to partner with.

Not long after, Kainos became a customer of ours and started to introduce content from Mindset (our self-coaching tool) and Lessons (our e-learning library) into the Effective Manager development programmes as pre-course learnings. It didn't stop there. To build capability and embed the learnings, the content was built upon and put into practice in workshops too. All the while, this was equipping managers to have better conversations, with the aim that coaching became part of everyday conversations.

The result has been brilliant, and that's why Kainos continues to partner with Coaching Culture year in, year out. The feedback about the blended programme has been tremendous. So much so, it's now offered around the globe. Not only that, but development for coaching conversations is not only offered to managers, but to leaders, project managers and Entry Level programmes too.

No wonder employee engagement scores have improved, customer satisfaction is at 98% and talent retention is at 92% (Kainos, October 2022).

"Coaching has become the air that we breathe and the primary skill for our people. Our programmes are a sell-out. And Coaching Culture's solutions are an important part of our success. Even though the solutions are easy to use, you offer so much more value and support. The relationship we have and the support you give is second to none. You're great at sharing best practice for how to engage our people with using the tools available. Working with Coaching Culture isn't just about buying an off-the-shelf solution – it's way more than that. You have content, resources, events and awards where we get to see what others are doing too. There's a whole lot more value added."

**Emma Lidgett, Head of Talent,
Development and Learning, Kainos Group PLC**

When managers adopt a coaching style more of the time, workplace magic starts to happen. To know we are making this level of difference to our customers and their employees around the world can only be described, quite simply, as a dream come true.

WHAT TO DO

Step 1: Define your coaching capability strategy

Depending on what your coaching capability strategy is, the solutions you will offer could be very different. In a coaching culture, everybody will have access to some level of coaching conversation, as only then can coaching and feedback become part of everyday life.

To be able to define your coaching capability strategy, it's important to understand what the current capability is in the organisation, where you want to get to, and what the gaps are.

Using an assessment tool will help to uncover coaching strengths and development areas to identify where the greatest need is. Also, having a clear vision of where you want to get to will determine which solutions best fit which capability need.

A popular route for many organisations is to offer coaching capability solutions as part of development programmes for leaders, managers, emerging talent, new starters, and project leaders. Others prefer to promote coaching solutions more widely to support those who may not be part of a development programme yet.

These could include formal coaching accreditations for internal coaches as well as digital coaching solutions available to all. One trap that organisations can fall into is providing a one-size-fits-all solution – in other words, the much-feared 'sheep-dip' approach.

That's why having a clear capability strategy defined, knowing who you want to develop, when and how is important. Only then can you offer the right solutions to the right people at the right time.

Like with any strategy, the coaching capability strategy must be dynamic, as progress is measured, feedback captured, and plans adapted accordingly.

Step 2: Identify your coaching capability solutions

Deciding which solutions to use in your organisation can be a minefield. Just put the words 'coaching capability solutions' or 'coaching culture solutions' into Google and you will see nearly 60 million results appear. While it can seem overwhelming, it really doesn't have to be.

Some organisations train their internal resources to deliver in-house coaching capability programmes, whereas others prefer to bring external support in. It's fair to say that they both have their pros and cons. What matters most is that you identify which type of solutions will add the most value to your organisational culture, strategy and budget, with a keen eye on the execution of the strategy and sustainability of the learnings. All too often, organisations seem to choose a solution to tick a box. Worse still, they simply apply a quick fix, like sticking a plaster over a wound.

For a coaching culture to be truly embedded, and for coaching to become *the* way to communicate, blended programmes are a positive step forward. Using the gift of time allows for change to be mentally processed, new ways of working to be practiced and applied, new habits formed, and behaviours changed for the long term. Whereas a quick fix solution is only ever that. A quick fix.

If budgets are a challenge, as they invariably are these days, digital solutions are a great way to achieve more with less. However, a blend of both digital and face-to-face solutions is stronger. Choosing a blend of solutions will ensure you provide the right support at the right time for the right audience.

Whether you are choosing to upskill your internal resource, or bring in external support to build coaching capability, reaching out to your trusted network on social media for recommendations is always a good place to start. No matter what, a positive word of mouth referral, alongside evidence of strong case studies, will give you the best chance of success.

Step 3: Build coaching capability

So, the coaching capability strategy has been created and it's time to execute the plan. It's important to ensure the people impacted by the strategy know what's coming. They need to be engaged, inspired and motivated to appreciate what's in it for them.

The magic starts to happen in an organisation when managers, who are already having conversations with their teams every day, start to use a coach approach more of the time. Rather than seeing it as an extra task added onto the day job, it *becomes* the day job.

I often say: 'To act like a coach, you have to be able to think like a coach.' In fact, it's one of my favourite sayings.

'Why is that?' you might be asking yourself. Well, because our thoughts and feelings drive our behaviours. So, to make sure managers can change their behaviours and develop new coaching habits, it makes sense to change their thoughts and feelings first. In other words, they have to develop a coach mindset.

Now you might be asking: 'Sounds fair, but what is a coach mindset?'

Again, another good question.

A coach mindset is when someone has an unconditional positive regard for others. In other words, they believe unconditionally in the other person. No matter what they say or do. A coach mindset is also someone who has enough self-awareness about their own thoughts, feelings, values and beliefs that they can recognise how their own behaviours may impact others. From there, they can then learn how to 'act like a coach' and develop the skills to adopt a coach approach more of the time.

The key to any successful coaching capability programme is to ensure time is provided to allow people to stop and think. To really reflect on their own behaviours and actions. It should not only focus on what could be driving those behaviours, but also what could be holding them back from unlocking even more potential in themselves and others. This will allow them to be able to develop their own coaching skills and have more effective conversations more of the time.

Once any coaching capability programmes start to be delivered, it's important to capture feedback along the way to ensure you continue to improve them all the time.

EXERCISE: TIME TO CHECK YOUR MANAGERS' SKILLS

The purpose of this exercise is to help you assess the different levels of coaching capability, either within your entire organisation or among certain groups. Knowing this information allows you to target the right coaching capability solutions to the right people. Invariably, capability will range from external accreditations to pockets of understanding of the G.R.O.W model to downright cynicism about coaching and everything in between. This exercise is best done through an assessment tool or survey sent to the audience that you would like to assess further. It's a bit like a learning needs analysis, when you figure out what learning solutions are required. Well, this is a coaching needs analysis, if you like.

1. **Decide which group of people you would like to assess.**

2. **Create the assessment survey, using the following questions as a guide:**

•   What is your role?

•   What coaching experience do you have?

    ▫   None

    ▫   Little experience

- Good experience

- Highly experienced

- Do you have an external accreditation? Yes/No

  - Which one?

- Do you have coaching conversations? Yes/No

- Who do you coach?

  - Your line manager and above

  - Team members

  - Peers

  - Direct reports

  - Self

  - Others

- How often do you have a coaching conversation?

  - Daily

  - Weekly

  - Monthly

  - Rarely

  - Never

- How would you rate your coaching conversations? (Scale of 1-10)

  □ 1 = ineffective, 10 = highly effective

- Do you use any coaching models to help structure your conversations? If so, which?

- How confident are you giving feedback?

  □ 1 = not confident, 10 = highly confident

- How comfortable are you at receiving feedback?

  □ 1 = very uncomfortable, 10 = very comfortable

- How confident at coaching are you?

  □ 1 = not confident, 10 = highly confident

3. **From a simple assessment, and depending on your strategy, you can decide what level of coaching capability is required per person or group of people.**

 HEAD TO JOWRIGHT.COM
TO DOWNLOAD MORE RESOURCES

TOP TEN TAKEAWAYS

In this chapter, we have learned:

1. To be able to act like a coach, you must be able to think like a coach.

2. A coach mindset is having an unconditional positive regard for others.

3. Developing your people is a vital step towards organisational success.

4. It's important to identify which coaching capability solutions are needed for which people.

5. The magic happens when managers adopt a coach approach more of the time.

6. Growing coaching capability is essential for organisations to succeed today and be fit for a successful tomorrow.

7. Caring for and trusting people has a direct correlation to the bottom line.

8. Command and control leadership is out of date.

9. Having a level of coaching capability is essential to being a people manager.

10. For a coaching culture to be truly embedded, longer-term blended programmes are a great solution.

CHAPTER 9

THRIVE

Unlock the power of feedback

"

———————————

Feedback is
the breakfast of
champions.

———————————

99

KEN BLANCHARD

MACHINE GUN FEEDBACK

t was the early 2000s. I was managing a sales team, a job I absolutely loved and felt proud to do. I really liked the team and enjoyed working with them. I'd not been on any meaningful management development programmes by that point. I just went with the flow and relied on being a decent human being to get the best out of people.

Or so I thought.

The time was coming up to the annual performance reviews. It was a time of year that, as a manager, I took very seriously. I saw it as my golden opportunity to have an honest and detailed conversation about everything that had happened in the previous 12 months. I put a lot of preparation into the conversation, and I expected my team to do the same. It was the least that we both could do to capture all the effort that had gone in and get any concerns that might be bubbling away onto the table. In fact, I'll be brutally honest, and I can still feel my stomach churning as I recount this story, it was way worse than that. I deliberately and intentionally chose to store all feedback up until the annual performance review, because that was the point of the reviews after all.

Again, or so I thought.

I hope you're starting to feel my pain as I write this.

I set up the review with one of my team. We already worked in a hybrid way, so we met in a hotel reception area, found a relatively quiet spot, grabbed some coffees, and set about the meeting.

The meeting was going well, and according to my clearly structured agenda, the time was drawing near for me to share my thoughts on what had and hadn't gone so well throughout the year. I took a deep breath and began to share my perspective. I got overly hung up on sharing my pent-up frustrations and focused way too much on what hadn't gone so well.

It wasn't even a shit sandwich. It was way worse. It was more like an AK47 machine gun firing out feedback bullets at a thousand rounds per minute.

After I had finished my so-called feedback and came up for air, an awkward silence fell over the corner of the reception area that we were nestled in.

I looked at my team member who had gone pale. He managed to compose himself, took a deep breath and mustered up the following words that he delivered with a shaky voice: 'I'M SHOCKED TO THE CORE. Why have you never told me this before?'

Those words have haunted me ever since.

Yet, at the same time, those words gave me one of the greatest career lessons of my life. In that very moment, a lightbulb went on in my brain and I remember to this day thinking: *What have I just done?*

I knew in that moment that I'd just crushed a valued member of my team right there. His face said it all. His words even more so. What an utter shit-show I'd just created.

From that moment on, I vowed never, ever again to save up feedback. Nor would I assume that if I'm thinking something, then others must be qualified mind-readers to read my thoughts.

WRONG! WRONG! WRONG!

While most people are intelligent, perceptive, intuitive even, what they are not, unless someone can prove otherwise, are mind-readers. And until that skill is mastered beyond all reasonable doubt, feedback must be given in-the-moment, or as timely as possible, in the most constructive of ways.

Please take the learnings from my valuable lesson because similar examples are still being provided by untrained, misguided and thoughtless managers in organisations today.

TURN UP THE DIAL

Needless to say, once the organisation is set up for having more coaching conversations, and confidence and capability are being built, it's time to turn up the feedback dial. What do I mean by that? It's time to push comfort zones and unlock the power of everyday feedback to raise organisational, team and self-awareness. And that's what this step of the framework is all about. How can the organisation grow and develop if it doesn't know what people are thinking and feeling? How can performance be enhanced without feedback along the way?

This can be done in many ways. On an organisational, team or individual level, using tools and techniques, such as feedback surveys and listening groups. Remember also, that some of the best conversations and insights are gathered in everyday conversations at the coffee machine and the water cooler too.

Gathering feedback will not only amplify what's great about the organisation, but it'll highlight any blind spots too. It will also serve to build an organisational growth mindset, unlock potential and ensure the organisation thrives.

Now this is where it can get uncomfortable for some. Gathering data and evidence for what is happening in the organisation and shining a light on areas that either need celebrating or improving can feel difficult. Nonetheless, it's invaluable data to help build the desired culture and develop high-performing teams and individuals. In fact, I'd go further than that. Successful people with a growth mindset proactively seek regular feedback, reflect on how they can improve and do something about it.

Coaching and feedback go hand in hand. A culture where coaching and feedback are part of everyday life is a healthy place to work. Asking questions, listening to understand, giving and receiving feedback, then acting upon it, are just some of the ingredients of building a coaching culture.

A DIVERSE CULTURAL TAPESTRY

This step of the framework is imperative when building a coaching culture. The benefits of giving and receiving feedback, whether on an organisational, team or individual level are endless. And whilst it can be difficult to both give and receive feedback, it's one of the most powerful ways to develop.

In a coaching culture, effective conversations and honest feedback are at the very core.

When done well, feedback helps to build trusting relationships, one of the main drivers of high performance. Thankfully, it is being increasingly recognised that meaningful relationships and having a true sense of connection and belonging are what make organisations tick.

We often talk about employee engagement, and rightly so. And whilst there's a strong link between feedback and employee engagement, unlocking the power of feedback runs way deeper than improving the all-important employee engagement metrics.

Organisations are made up of people. They don't just come to work with a brain, they come with a busy mind and a full heart too. Putting this altogether on an organisational level creates a complex mix of thoughts, feelings, emotions and behaviours. When harnessed brilliantly, this creates a unique and diverse cultural tapestry, made up of creativity, innovation and high performance.

People are at the heart of every organisation. People matter. And so do their thoughts, opinions and ideas. They should be valued. Cherished even. Getting inside the mind of the organisation and then observing how well the heart of the organisation is beating needs to be checked and monitored regularly. If left unchecked, the overall cultural health of the organisation can start to deteriorate.

Measuring how the organisation and teams are progressing on several important topics (such as engagement, trust, wellbeing, inclusivity and communication) and regularly being able to gather insights will allow issues or themes to be highlighted and addressed at pace.

This also is true for individual feedback. Promoting a culture where feedback is expected and respected and delivered as regularly as possible helps to embed a healthy culture of open and honest communication, creating a sense of wellbeing and belonging, building trust and high performance. Not only that, but newer generations of employees expect to receive regular feedback. In fact, they crave it. They want to be asked for their ideas and opinions, they want to give their feedback, they want to feel valued. They are unlike the generations before them, who were more known for waiting to be told what to do, avoiding feedback like the plague and just getting their heads down to take a wage. How times have changed.

In fact, the extent to which times have changed mustn't be underestimated. Times have changed and continue to change at a rapid pace, and can be summed up by this fabulous quote:

> *"The rate of change today is faster than it's ever been, but it's never going to be this slow again."*

Chris van der Kuyl CBE

TALKING WITH THEIR FEET

Employees don't need to hang around anymore in organisations that aren't meeting their needs. The global pandemic created a new era of organisational control. We are seeing a much needed and significant shift of power from employer to employee. When the days of employers barking 'jump' and employees responding with 'how high?' are long gone. Well, almost. I say 'almost' because clearly this is not the case in every organisation.

The pandemic provided valuable and deep reflective time for many people. Lost in their own thoughts, they realised that they couldn't see loved ones when they wanted to. They recognised that without our health, we have nothing. They acknowledged that life and work are intrinsically linked. Aside from all the heartache and anxiety that the pandemic initiated, we are likely to have just experienced one of the greatest connections to personal values in our lifetime.

No wonder this has led to a chain of new phrases being coined to describe what's going on in the world of work. The great re-evaluation, the great resignation, the great power shift, quiet quitting, loud leaving and who knows what next? It's hardly surprising to learn that the number of employees who left their roles in the UK in 2021 was at a record high, and it depended on how their employer treated them throughout the pandemic. It's time for organisations to wake up and smell the coffee. Employees are talking with their feet.

For those who haven't resigned and headed to more purposeful employers, they may now be sat working from home acting their wage. In other words, doing the minimum required to get by each day. Remember those zombies I mentioned in Chapter 7? The employees who are neither fully dead nor fully alive? Well, the toxic organisations are breeding grounds for them right now. If ever there was a word of warning for every organisation that doesn't have its ear to the ground or its finger on the organisational pulse, it's right there. Replacing lost talent is an avoidable and high price to pay indeed.

CASE STUDY: IMPELLAM GROUP PLC

Impellam is a connected group providing global workforce and specialist recruitment solutions, operating nine brands across the world. Three years ago, it was recognised that one of the drivers of global success was the need to embed coaching and feedback across the leadership and management population. At the time, the organisation was at a stage where feedback mainly took place in a manager one-to-one conversation. Yet there was a realisation that the leadership and management population couldn't raise their self-awareness and develop without an understanding of what other people thought of them. And with the aspiration to build a culture of feedback, where people felt psychologically safe to give and receive feedback, it needed to be given and received in all directions. Up, down and sideways.

It was a bold goal for sure.

> *"We needed to have honest conversations.*
> *As only from a position of truth could we*
> *move forwards."*

Lucy Scally, Performance
and Development Business Partner

To achieve this, the team at Impellam knew feedback needed to be given and received in line with the organisational behavioural framework, 'Virtuosity'. They needed to find a provider who would be happy to work in partnership with them to create cost-effective feedback solutions to perfectly suit their needs.

Soon after, they met the Coaching Culture team at the Learning Technologies exhibition in London. Not only did they find the solutions that met their needs, but they recognised we were a group of people that they could work closely with.

And the rest is history, as they say.

Shortly afterwards, Impellam became a valued customer of Coaching Culture's. They have been using Mindset (our self-coaching tool) and Lessons (our eLearning library) as well as our feedback tool.

Mindset, the self-coaching tool, helps individuals to raise their self-awareness and to self-coach on areas such as emotional intelligence, change readiness, creativity, and growth mindset. Yet, to meet Impellam's needs, it was important to not just raise self-awareness, but to get feedback from other people on the same areas. So, working with Coaching Culture, further surveys, which were aligned to the Virtuosity framework, were created and launched.

Managers increasingly ask for specific and targeted feedback from colleagues, team members and other stakeholders. Further raising their awareness, challenging their personal perceptions, and giving them key insights into how others perceive them in their role. A brave move, but an essential one in a people-led organisation.

So, what has been the outcome?

Well, from a place where feedback was just being given in manager one-to-ones, and with the ongoing use of feedback tools, Impellam are now in a place where more than 576 managers are giving and receiving feedback regularly. One of the brands has even targeted and rewarded managers on the number of feedback surveys that they request.

While creating a culture of feedback is an ongoing work-in-progress, they are very proud of how far they have come. Targeted feedback is being given and received across different stakeholders, and teams are now regularly being asked for feedback. All of this has created new opportunities across the business and broadened the general field of vision. The aspiration is that the Coaching Culture solutions will be expanded across the whole organisation. But like so many of our customers know, to build a culture of coaching and feedback takes time. Nonetheless, it's important to start somewhere.

"Everyone we have met at Coaching Culture is like one of us. The team at Coaching Culture is equally passionate about coaching and feedback, and they share our vision. There is a true understanding of our business. Coaching Culture have continued to bring us practical solutions and support that works. It's a true partnership."

Lucy Scally, Performance and Development Business Partner

Listening to Lucy share the Impellam story was a proud moment for me, for sure. In particular, the way she spoke about our Head of Customer Success, Sharon Woods, and how she worked tirelessly to deliver what Impellam required, was a delight to hear. I instantly jumped onto our own conversations platform to thank and praise Sharon.

Why?

Because feedback matters.

WHAT TO DO

Step 1: Define your feedback strategy

The most successful organisations ensure that the opportunity to give and receive feedback is continuous. As an organisation, it's important to have a feedback strategy, so it's clear what type of feedback is given, by who and when. This will range from organisation-wide surveys, group and team surveys, and listening groups to one-to one feedback. All of it provides highly valuable data about what's going on in the minds of your employees.

It's common to execute in-depth organisational surveys once or twice a year, which can prove to be an unwieldy process. Gathering feedback on all areas of the business to measure employee engagement and satisfaction is important. The key is doing something about the rich data that is returned.

To complement these, the light touch weekly pulse surveys are becoming increasingly common. These may simply ask a handful of questions and only take a couple of minutes to complete. They are far easier to execute and can highlight any themes and trends that may be arising early on. Many organisations I speak to do a weekly pulse check. Importantly, the responses tend to form a valuable discussion point with the senior leadership team every week.

Drilling down further to understand certain groups, teams or individuals is another valuable way to unlock the power of feedback. This could be done through surveys, listening groups, 360 feedback campaigns and regular one-to-one meetings. High-performing teams and individuals have the strength of character to ask for feedback regularly, reflect and learn from it. It becomes habitual. Not something that happens once or twice a year.

Choosing the right systems, tools and platforms to put in place, as well as building the capability to have honest conversations, will ensure that feedback can become a powerful part of everyday life.

Step 2: Implement the feedback strategy

Giving and receiving feedback can feel a challenge for many people. It's important to understand whether transparent feedback or anonymous feedback will get the best result. While organisation-wide transparent feedback would be the ideal goal, it relies on a high degree of psychological safety already being in place. Let's face it, people are more open when they trust they can give their honest thoughts and feelings without fear of retribution.

In a coaching culture, feedback is part of everyday life. It's expected and respected. Where you are on your cultural journey will dictate how you will go about executing your feedback strategy.

The careful positioning and framing of why feedback is being requested, as well as highlighting the benefits, is key. Reassuring people that their honesty matters and their opinions are valued will help to build trust.

It's not as simple as just saying to people, 'Hey everyone, it's feedback time. Let's do this thing!' Making sure that people have the confidence and capability to give and receive feedback is important. Many organisations run workshops, masterclasses and bite-sized lunch and learn sessions on this very subject. The more confidence that people have to be able to share their honest opinions, the more successful the organisation will become, and the less oxygen is given to the potential pity parties.

Implementing your feedback strategy and regularly evaluating how it's going is important. The more the organisational feedback muscles are built, when feedback is asked for and welcomed, the greater the cultural impact all round.

Step 3: Listen to understand

All feedback is data. Data from which you can gather valuable insights, highlighting areas of strength and potential blind spots. Having insight means you can make decisions on the back of it. Feedback is priceless.

Nonetheless, the most important part of any level of organisational team or individual feedback is when you listen to what is being said and what's not. Understanding the feedback more deeply and doing something about it is vital. I can't emphasise this point enough.

'You said, we did' or 'You said, we didn't, because...' is a super-powerful strategy to adopt in any organisation. Too many times, this is the point where the strategy crumbles in both execution and cred-ibility. When organisations gather the feedback that employees have taken the time to give, what happens then? Nothing happens. Nada. Diddly squat. That's simply not good enough, I'm afraid.

Let's call it out for what it is. Lazy and damaging. How often have you been told that people aren't completing the organisational surveys 'because nothing ever changes'. This is the all-important 'so what?' and 'now what?' part of the strategy. This is the time when you circle back around and advise what may or may not change on the back of any employee feedback.

Listening groups are a great way to facilitate a deeper understand-ing of any organisational surveys, provided they are set up as a psychologically safe space to talk. These are often facilitated by external facilitators as they are seen as impartial. If budgets don't allow for this, then it's often carried out by representatives from the People team.

For smaller feedback campaigns, group, team, and individual coaching sessions are powerful ways to follow up on any feedback shared. They provide space for reflection, for feedback to be pro-cessed, new perspectives to be considered and action plans to be agreed.

No matter how you decide to follow up on feedback, listening to understand, coaching people through feedback and creating action plans will continue to build trust and high performance as a result. No wonder it's such a vital step.

EXERCISE: PUT YOUR EAR TO THE GROUND

The purpose of this exercise is to give you the tools to carry out a listening group. Confident facilitation and careful navigation of this session will add credibility to the whole feedback process.

1. Decide which group of people you would like to speak to and why. Having a clear purpose and desired outcome of the session is key to its success.

2. Plan the session in some detail. It's important to plan how you intend to introduce the session, the topics you would like to cover, the questions that will get you to the desired outcomes and how much time you anticipate for each topic.

3. Invite the participants to the listening group, clearly explaining the purpose of the session. The session should ideally be 90 minutes or so. This allows enough time for healthy debate, while remaining short enough to stay highly focused.

4. Set up the session with clear contracting expectations and guidelines to ensure conversations are confidential and honest, allowing for a constructive and productive session all round. Share what will happen to the information gathered and the next steps.

5. Role-modelling coaching skills throughout is important. Make sure everyone is included and that no one person dominates the session.

6. Facilitate the session with empathy, while you carefully navigate towards the goal of the session.

7. Thank the group for participating. Make sure you leave them feeling listened to and that their opinions are valued.

8. Most importantly, enjoy the opportunity that this presents. You get to deeply listen to understand the people who are working at the sharp end.

9. Always share the agreed actions after the session. The technique of 'you said, we did' works really well.

10. While it's not always possible to accommodate every request or suggestion that comes through, remember to include 'you said, we didn't, because…' as a valuable way to acknowledge you've listened and you're being transparent about the decision-making process.

Remember, when you make the time to put your ear to the ground and listen to the people within the organisation, the insight you will gather will be priceless.

 HEAD TO JOWRIGHT.COM
TO DOWNLOAD MORE RESOURCES

TOP TEN TAKEAWAYS

In this chapter, we have learned:

1. Regular feedback is invaluable. It helps to build the culture, high-performing teams and individuals.

2. The most successful organisations, teams and individuals ask for feedback regularly.

3. In a coaching culture, feedback is expected and respected.

4. Coaching and feedback go hand in hand.

5. Honest feedback builds trusting relationships and high performance.

6. When people can share their thoughts, opinions and ideas, they feel heard and valued.

7. For some, giving and receiving feedback can feel uncomfortable. Practice building the organisational feedback muscle through workshops and masterclasses.

8. There are several ways to gather feedback: surveys, feedback campaigns, listening groups, one-to-one meetings and everyday conversations.

9. It's important to regularly check in on the organisational climate.

10. The most important part of a feedback strategy is when it is listened to and acted upon. The techniques of 'you said, we did' or 'you said, we didn't, because…' work well.

CHAPTER 10

PERFORM

Build trust and drive high performance

"

If you have a goal,
write it down. If you
don't write it down,
it's just a wish.

"

STEVE MARABOLDI

CLEAR AS MUD

'How are you getting on with speaking to Sarah and James? Have they been supportive?' I asked Mike.

Mike was one of my more experienced Learning and Development Managers. We got on well. We understood each other. He knew his stuff, but most importantly, he had a can-do attitude. And some. I liked that in him. On reflection, I probably saw myself in him: always wanting to impress, wanting to help others, wanting to succeed. They were the kind of qualities I admired in people.

'Sarah and James?' Mike asked, as his brow furrowed, and he looked back at me with an unnervingly confused expression.

'You know. When I suggested that you catch up with them to give you feedback on the programme you've been designing?'

Silence… Mike's confused expression deepened.

In my mind, I started to wonder where my explanation was going wrong. I thought I'd try again, to add more clarity to my woolly communication.

'Remember? In our last one-to-one, we discussed the management development programme you've been designing. An action was that you would go and speak with Sarah and James to get their thoughts and feedback.'

I quickly scrambled around in my notebook, looking for my scribbled notes that I took in the meeting a month ago. It's often been suggested that maybe I had been a doctor in a former life, based upon my illegible writing.

'A-ha! Found them!' I said out loud and quietly smiled to myself. I had a point to prove, if nothing else; I had to prove the conversation had indeed taken place, and I wasn't losing my mind.

I looked down at my scribbled notes, slightly dismayed at their illegibility, but happy they were there nonetheless.

'Saneh…Janee…fdbk: MT action.'

Well, that was clear. Clear as mud.

I shared my scribbled notes with Mike.

'There,' I said, proudly pointing to my handwritten notes.

Mike glanced down at my notes for what seemed like an age, while his confused expression remained steadfast.

He then looked up. I watched as his eyes darted to the left and right, searching inside his brain for some sort of vague recollection of the conversation. Suddenly, his facial expression started to change as the memory slowly started to creep back into his conscious mind.

'Aaaaaah, yeah, I remember now.' Mike's discomfort was visibly building as he realised that he'd totally forgotten to get their feedback. 'Shit, Jo, I've not done it. I totally forgot.'

I respected his honesty.

It was a pretty important step in the design phase of our programmes, getting stakeholder feedback. The very people whose teams would be taking part and being developed through the programme. And the deadline for the completion of the programme design was looming.

Damn, I silently thought.

'It's not ideal,' I said. 'But it's not the end of the world either.'

Which was true. I had a healthy grip on reality at this stage of my career. As far as I was concerned, only the end of the world was indeed the end of the world, and it was important to remember that whenever the pressure was piling on.

My notes were just a mass of scribbles. We'd finished the previous meeting hastily as time had run out, and consequently, we'd not confirmed our agreed actions. Instead, I had grabbed my book, my pen, and my bag, and rushed off to the next meeting, leaving an air of unfinished business. I'd not sent any follow-on notes, because that would have felt too formal. It was just a verbal conversation between two professionals, with some hastily scribbled notes.

It made me reflect.

So many learning opportunities right there.

What one person had said, and assumed had been agreed, was not what had been agreed at all. Worse than that, it had been left to scribbled notes, recollections of vague memories leaving everything to chance and zero accountability. I silently berated myself for my failed communication efforts, and the following quote by Richard Bandler, the founder of Neuro Linguistic Programming, bounced around my head like a game of pinball:

'The meaning of communication is the response you get.'

My below-par communication effort had resulted in this.

Thankfully, that specific error was quickly sorted, and the feedback from Sarah and James was gathered. But the lesson was far greater. Lessons in communication, task management, note-taking, accountability. All of which would have been rectified by the effective capturing of the conversation.

END OF THE ANNUAL APPRAISAL

This step is one of the final keys to unlock the power of coaching and feedback and to really start to unlock high performance. Building on the previous steps, where capability has been developed, feedback is becoming part of everyday life and the benefit of trusting relationships is becoming apparent.

This step is when coaching conversations become the way to communicate and manage performance. Building rapport, asking questions, listening, setting goals, giving feedback, and creating accountability ensures individuals, teams and the entire organisation perform at the highest level.

It's the step when coaching expectations are truly embraced. Furthermore, policies, procedures and platforms are introduced to ensure that everybody is behind the organisational vision to build a coaching culture.

This is the time to be bold. To redefine the old school way of performance management and replace the time-consuming and dreaded annual performance reviews with everyday conversations.

This is the time to replace unreliable spreadsheets to capture goals, set fire to the manager one-to-one notebooks and confidently embrace efficient technology to do the hard work.

This is the time to introduce a tool that captures goals and objectives, captures conversations and actions, encourages regular feedback, and continues to develop coaching capability. Not only that, but such tools also remove the reliance on memory and increase the efficiency and effectiveness of everyday conversations. It's essential at a time when the role of the manager is getting ever more challenging, and the pace of life is getting quicker.

EMBRACING TECHNOLOGY

This step of the framework is important when building a coaching culture. The benefits of communicating effectively, capturing key points from conversations, and creating a sense of accountability are essential for high performance. So much in life boils down to effective communication. It's easy to say, but not always easy to do.

Using such tools and capturing relevant notes and information allows the necessary people to keep abreast of organisational progress at the touch of a button. They no longer need to chase around for spreadsheets from functional heads. Instead, the important insights and data are available and at hand, in an instant.

Organisational goal setting, team and individual objectives, everyday coaching conversations, in-the-moment feedback, personal development plans, they can all be captured in one efficient system. Clarity of expectations, honest communication and mutually agreed action points allow for more effective management of performance. All of it provides rich data and insights and better-informed decision-making like never before.

No longer is it acceptable for the People teams to be making important decisions based on 'they said this' and 'they said that'. Or for decisions to be based on some random notes captured on a word document, saved in a secret file on somebody's creaking computer. It's imperative in the 21st century to stay abreast of the technological landscape and move with the times.

Views on how performance is managed in organisations is rapidly changing, so too has the technology that supports it.

Time and time again, it's been proven that employees today are expecting more from their managers. Greater clarity of role expectations, honest and regular feedback on how they are performing, an interest and genuine care in their overall wellbeing. Up until recent times, managers have been trusted to have those conversations.

Now the technology is available to not only provide the evidence that such conversations are indeed happening, but also the most relevant developmental support, at the time of need, to ensure the conversations are meaningful, effective and captured as efficiently as possible.

Knowing that the conversations are happening and that employees are receiving honest and timely feedback in a consistent way also allows for calibration meetings and reward and recognition conversations to be evidence-based, with no shocks or surprises for the employee.

Ensuring these honest conversations and practices become the norm will also directly impact employee motivation, engagement and performance and allow for more effective data-driven decisions. Not only that, but such systems and tools should help to reduce the number of times that the People teams run around feeling like their backsides are on fire.

OK, so we can but dream.

THE DIGITAL ERA

Only time will tell for those organisations who don't move with the times and join many other successful organisations who are leading the way by using effective performance management tools. They are becoming an expected tool to optimise performance in this age of technology. Well, certainly by the more people-focussed, forward-thinking organisations.

Can we truly imagine a world where we go back to relying on pen and paper, hastily scribbled notes, vague recollections and random spreadsheets? Not in a million years. The digital era, thankfully, is here to stay.

Global communities are developing quickly, and communication can be quicker and more effective than ever. No wonder workplace efficiencies are part and parcel of such glorious advancements in technology. Nonetheless, this isn't only about efficiencies – it's way more than that. These tools help to promote regular conversations that build trust. They provide individuals the space to learn and grow, capturing personal reflections and two-way feedback.

They help to build a culture where coaching conversations are the norm. They become *the* way to communicate and manage performance.

The cost of not building a culture where employees know what is expected of them, where their managers help them to grow and develop, will prove costly in terms of financial performance, but in all other People metrics too. An organisation on a downward spiral is not a healthy organisation. An organisation like that will keep People teams more than busy working on solving issues that could have been avoided through effective communication.

CASE STUDY: RESTORE PLC

Back in October 2020, Louisa joined Restore PLC as the Head of Leadership, Talent and Culture. Restore is one of the UK's leading providers of data, information, and asset management services, and it is made up of five business units. When Louisa joined Restore, the world was still in the middle of a global pandemic. While the rest of the world was still wondering how to lead through a pandemic, the People team at Restore knew there'd never been a better time to focus on culture and performance management.

Interestingly, at that time, Restore's five business units were starting to join forces to be more efficient. This brought challenge and opportunity in equal measures. On the one hand, there was the challenge of bringing together different processes, on the other, it provided an opportunity to try new ways of working. One of those ways included ditching the annual appraisal in favour of regular conversations, goal-setting and continuous feedback. One of the business unit Heads of People had seen it happen in a previous company and had experienced the successes first hand. And while they successfully implemented the process and behaviours, the problem was that there was no 'digital home' for capturing the regular conversations.

By chance, Louisa stumbled across Coaching Culture's conversations platform, which was at the early stages of development in the innovation incubator. To quote Louisa: 'The universe responded. It was exactly what we needed to support this business unit.'

As such early adopters, it gave the team at Restore the unique opportunity to create a solution that perfectly met their needs. No wonder Restore have become such a critical and valued partner. They have worked hand in hand with us to develop the conversations platform into the fabulous solution that it is today.

Nonetheless, as we know, just because a solution is developed, it doesn't guarantee user-adoption. Work still had to be done.

As one business unit started to use and love the platform, the jungle drums started to beat, and the good word got out. Through their 'Leading at Restore' programme, leaders across the business got to hear about the new enjoyable way of setting goals, capturing conversations, giving and receiving feedback and building confidence through the library of bite-sized content.

A year down the line and all five business units are well on their way to fully adopting the platform without it being overly pushed. A welcome new digital home for conversations has been found. Not only that, but the annual appraisal has officially been laid to rest, providing more effective time and space to have continuous conversations focusing on people and performance.

A shining example of starting small, then expanding over time.

To top it off, the feedback has been phenomenal.

"You are a fantastic organisation, with a real passion for creating something that makes a difference. Your purpose is clear, and it's an absolute pleasure to work with you. The team at Coaching Culture and the coaching conversations platform are fantastic, and you respond so well to feedback. The product has come on massively; it's so easy to use and intuitive. I've thoroughly enjoyed working with you to develop something that will make a difference to so many."

**Louisa Fryer, Head of Leadership,
Talent and Culture, Restore PLC**

To hear those words spoken out loud by a highly respected People professional makes me beam with pride. Our purpose is 'to make work better', so to hear Louisa describe the impact that we are having is why we do what we do.

WHAT TO DO

Step 1: Assess your performance management systems and processes

To be a truly high-performing organisation, effective conversations and feedback must be integrated into the organisational systems, policies and procedures. In other words, to build a coaching culture, people need to be fully supported within an organisational framework. They need to know what is expected of them, what good looks like and how they can truly thrive.

It's all too easy to simply make assumptions about how people are going about the day job. The only real way to find out is by asking the question. So, lift the bonnet of the organisation and have a good look underneath. It's a great place to start.

Auditing the organisation can be done through surveys, interviews with key stakeholders and listening groups. Having the data and evidence about what is happening on a day-to-day basis is an impactful way to identify what still needs to be done.

Questions such as:

- Do you know the vision, purpose and goals of the business?

- Do you know how your role aligns to the overall strategy?

- How do you currently measure performance?

- How do you currently manage performance?

- How do you currently communicate?

- How often do you have one-to-ones?

- How is performance measured?

- How are goals and objectives set?

- Where are goals and objectives captured?

- How is progress measured?

- How is feedback shared?

- How are regular actions documented?

- How are you rated?

- How are you rewarded and recognised?

Now, don't get me wrong, looking under the bonnet at this stage can uncover all sorts of areas: different ways of working, different systems, different functions doing different things.

As time has gone by and new people have brought in their new ideas from previous companies, unbeknown to them, and with all good intentions, they may have added to the organisational confusion.

While that may be OK for some, it's not the most efficient way for an organisation to operate in anyone's book. When people have clarity in regard to what is expected of them in their role, have the right tools to do a great job and have the support systems around them, only then can they and the organisation begin to flourish.

Step 2: Decide on how you want to manage performance

Once you have audited what is currently happening and what currently exists in the organisation, you can decide what you want to happen going forward. The size of the opportunity will depend on what the audit has uncovered, what is needed and the appetite for change. It's likely to vary by team, department or function, depending on the size of the organisation.

Looking around and researching how other successful organisations manage their performance is a great indicator as to what great looks like and what works. Common denominators include: clarity of goals, regular one-to-ones, regular feedback and honest conversations, supported by technology. Yes, you've got it. The organisations who have a coaching culture.

By clarifying how you want to manage and measure performance it will give you every chance of organisational success. Only when you know where you want to go, can you put the right systems and processes in place to get you there.

Step 3: Define a plan to manage performance

Once you have decided where you want to go, and how you want to manage performance, only then can you plan how you are going to achieve it.

Several organisations have started to introduce coaching and feedback policies, stating how often one-to-ones need to take place, with guidelines on how to conduct them. These are not separate coaching tasks added onto the usual one-to-ones. They are the one-to-ones. If coaching is to become the way to communicate, encouraging in-the-moment feedback and regular conversations is the way forward. Consider what you'd want your own policies to be.

More and more organisations are replacing the need for annual appraisals. They are removing the unwieldy painstaking process that it has become in favour of regular conversations and feedback. Why? Because regular communication and small, incremental improvements through regular feedback allows for any course correction, building greater trust and high performance as a result. A review, once or twice a year, isn't the answer. Is this the time to make a change? Testing this in a small area, or with one function, to capture learnings and feedback, is the most common step forward towards making larger-scale change later down the line.

As coaching and feedback becomes more common, choosing the right platform to capture goals, objectives and continuous feedback is important. Relying on word documents, personal notebooks, spreadsheets and memory is outdated at best, inefficient at worst.

Using technology to capture goals, conversations and feedback is not meant to interrupt the flow of a meaningful conversation. It's meant to enhance the effectiveness of conversations to ensure clarity of communication, measure progress and capture feedback. Our customers particularly love the fact that our conversation platform also allows for self-reflection, continuous feedback and development solutions at the point of need.

EXERCISE: PLAN TO PERFORM

The purpose of this exercise is to help you shape your performance management plan. In most organisations, it's the responsibility of the People team to have researched the market and defined what best practice is.

Creating the plan itself is best done as a workshop between a small number of stakeholders, led by the People team with representatives from other functions.

Performance management strategy workshop

1. **Choose the right people to be in the room**

2. **Answer the following questions as a group, and agree the way forward:**

- How do we want to share the vision, purpose and goals of the business?

- How do we want to share how roles align to the overall strategy?

- How do we want to measure performance?

- How do we want to manage performance?

- How do we want to communicate?

- How often do we want to have one-to-ones?

- How do we want goals and objectives to be set?

- How do we want goals and objectives to be captured?

- How do we want to measure progress?

- How do we want feedback to be shared?

- How do we want to capture regular actions?

- How do we want to measure people?

- How do we want to reward and recognise?

- How do we want to implement a plan?

- How do we want to measure progress against the plan?

3. Create a performance management plan on a page

Following on from the workshop and the agreed way forward, it's time to document this in a one-page plan. It would ideally include the following headlines:

- Vision

- Goals

- Objectives

- Measures of success

- Key milestones

- Resources

HEAD TO JOWRIGHT.COM
TO DOWNLOAD MORE RESOURCES

TOP TEN TAKEAWAYS

In this chapter, we have learned:

1. The meaning of communication is the response that you get.

2. The role of the manager is becoming increasingly challenging.

3. The time has come to redefine performance management.

4. Annual performance reviews can be effectively replaced by regular conversations and feedback.

5. To measure performance effectively, people must be clear about what is expected of them.

6. Technology can enable more efficient and effective conversations.

7. Effective communication and creating a sense of accountability are essential for high performance.

8. Data-driven insights allow for better informed decision-making.

9. Better conversations lead to greater trust and higher performance.

10. Test in a small area to capture learnings in advance of larger scale change.

CHAPTER 11

SUSTAIN

Embed a
coaching culture

"

If you get the
culture right,
most of the other
stuff will take
care of itself.

"

TONY HSIEH

WONDER WOMAN

I t was that dreaded time of year again: the annual appraisal. This time I was the one under scrutiny. Or at least that's how it felt to me.

My manager was relatively new. He seemed a decent enough guy, but there was something about him that left me with a slight feeling of unease when I was in his company. I couldn't quite put my finger on it at the time. He was professional, came with great credentials and had made a pretty good first impression with all those that he had encountered so far. But, for me, there was just something I didn't quite trust. Call it intuition. Call it a gut feeling. I didn't quite know what it was at the time.

On reflection, if I was to call it out now, I think it was probably the fact he walked around telling anybody who would listen that he had been brought into the organisation to be eventually promoted into his boss's shoes, the most senior role in the People function. It was like there was a blatant disregard for his team's development needs and ambitions. On reflection, it was more than that. It was the fact that he shared his career aspirations with a superior air, leaving me feeling like I had the threat of 'Either you're with me, or you're not' hanging over my head.

It was that.

Me, me, me. Not we, we, we.

Anyway, the time had come for that awkward moment of review-ing the full year that had passed by in a heartbeat, despite us having only worked together for six months. Up until this point, we'd had a couple of one-to-ones where we had got to know each other a bit better, and the feedback to me had never been anything other than glowing.

I had prepared well for the meeting. It was that time of year that my pay rise would be confirmed, and the bonus would be allocated. I was hoping for a healthy bonus, as the business was doing well, and my contribution to that was clear in the results. Not only that, but the incentive of a decent bonus linked to a job well done had been one of the carrots that had been dangled throughout the year when I was tirelessly travelling up and down the country with a blatant disregard to the impact on my personal life.

We started the conversation, and it was going well. I'd gathered evidence and feedback from both my key stakeholders and my team, and I lined up proof after proof of the results the team and I had been delivering, as well as the all-round decent job I was doing. My hopes were high for that decent pay rise and bonus.

As I took a breath, and was about to carry on with more dazzling evidence, my line manager blurted out: 'You're meeting expectations.'

'Sorry?' I said, in a questioning tone.

'You're just meeting expectations.'

The words 'meeting expectations' rang inside my ears. It was made worse by the addition of one of the most demeaning words in the English language: the word 'just'. Was I only JUST meeting expectations by the skin of my teeth? Or was I JUST meeting expectations rather than reaching the dizzying heights of 'exceeding expectations' (which was the next one up the performance rankings scale)?

JUST.

MEETING.

EXPECTATIONS.

Wow. I thought. Just wow.

I sat back in my seat, taking in the feedback, like I had been slapped in the face.

'But I've worked my backside off all year,' I hastily justified.

My line manager looked down at his hands, while awkwardly twiddling with his shiny Mont Blanc pen. 'To be honest, Jo, I appreciate what you're saying, but the decision has already been made. I've got to work within the pay review distribution curve. The forced distribution curve.'

All my evidence and feedback gathering felt like a giant waste of time as my line manager had already decided with the other powers-that-be that I was meeting expectations. Sorry. I mean, JUST meeting expectations.

So much for a healthy bonus. Dreams of taking the kids to Disney in Florida were becoming less and less likely. I told myself that a trip to Alton Towers in the heart of rural England would be just as good fun. Just. That damn word again.

Why was I feeling so surprised? Shocked even. Because all the conversations that we'd had up until this point had all been pointing towards the direction of 'Jo the superstar' who was exceeding expectations. I questioned whether I had been denying the signs that I was just meeting expectations throughout, but I knew I hadn't. All the words of affirmation and positive feedback I had received along the way told me that I wasn't deluded. 'Overworked and a bit of a mug' was definitely more accurate.

I felt let down and embarrassed that I'd given my everything to this organisation for a good while now. For what? To be told I was just meeting expectations.

If only my manager had been clear throughout the year what exceeding expectations would have looked like on the pay and bonus scale. If only my manager had been honest along the way, not just dishing out positive words to make me feel good. It left me wondering whether even Wonder Woman would have managed to exceed expectations on his pre-determined unattainable distribution curve. The small amount of trust that had been building disappeared in a heartbeat.

MEANINGFUL CONVERSATIONS

The focus here is on building upon the previous steps. At this point, capability has been developed, honest feedback is becoming part of everyday life, coaching conversations are becoming the way to communicate, and the organisation has effective systems and processes in place to manage performance.

This step is the final step to embed a coaching culture when managers role-model the desired behaviours every step of the way. This is where they continue to develop a coaching culture that builds trust and drives high performance.

This step is when it is all brought together. Managers are championing and role-modelling effective coaching conversations on an ongoing basis, helping their teams to truly thrive whilst making sure they sustain new behaviours and embed the desired culture.

This is the point where it feels positive to work in the organisation; you can look around and see, hear and feel the difference. The teams are buzzing due to meaningful work and healthy collaborations. Successes are shared and celebrated. Coaching conversations are permeating throughout the organisation. Personal development is evident and organisation-wide creativity is happening, as if by magic. The organisation is growing and succeeding. There's a healthy vibe around the place and, if any issues arise, they are swiftly addressed and with great integrity.

This step is when you just know that you are working in an environment that is setting people up not only to succeed but to flourish. Here there are no surprises because annual appraisals are a thing of the past, and everyday conversations are enabling continuous feedback and improvements for growth. Meaningful conversations are a habit.

TWO STEPS FORWARDS

This step is all about sticking to the plan. Believing in the plan. Overcoming obstacles along the way. Moving two steps forwards, one step back. After all, moving towards the strategic north star of a coaching culture requires grit and determination. The importance of implementing and refining the strategy, rather than ripping it up and starting again, is clear. The all too familiar 'initiativitus' that permeates too many organisations needs to be avoided. The time when ideas are agreed upon, when a new person joins the business full of enthusiasm and impressive experiences, offers an opportunity. However, the ideas are executed poorly, then they are simply abandoned when the next person flies through the revolving door.

The benefits of a coaching culture are well documented.

Positive metrics shine in areas including:

1. Talent attraction and retention

2. Employee engagement

3. Customer satisfaction

4. Wellbeing

5. Inclusivity

6. Creativity and innovation

7. Trust and psychological safety

8. Financial performance

There are simply no downsides to building a coaching culture. Not one.

We know it's more important than ever. The post-pandemic research and employee feedback is firmly pointing to a healthy culture and workplace being the way to succeed in the 21st century and beyond.

For those in the People team, such positive metrics make work better for all employees, and that includes them too. One of the greatest benefits for building a coaching culture is the shift of responsibility and accountability over to managers to coach their teams to achieve the organisational, team and individual goals.

The baton is handed over to ensure they take responsibility for creating the environment for their teams to flourish. The People team become enablers of change, allowing them to get rid of the feeling that they must *be* everything to all people and *do* everything too.

This becomes a very empowering place to be. Partnering with managers, providing them with the resources and tools to succeed, rather than running around doing the job for them. When you enable and empower others to develop, by default, you grow too. It's a virtuous cycle. Building a coaching culture is a win-win all round.

HUMAN SUFFERING

The cost of not building a coaching culture is a heavy one.

If a coaching culture is a place where authentic leaders and managers help people to grow, thrive and perform through effective conversations and honest feedback, underpinned by trust, then what would be the opposite of that? A toxic culture full of dysfunctional teams, that's what.

Research has proven that the cost of toxic cultures runs into the billions across the globe. That's the cost of high absenteeism, loss of talent, poor productivity, fear, burn out and unhealthy working environments. Driven by toxic behaviours such as back-stabbing, aggression, micro-management, lack of accountability, gaslighting, bullying and blaming others. The list goes on…

If you don't provide the time, space and resources for building a healthy culture, then that's what will happen. It's a vicious downward spiral from there. A culture of negativity and low trust will prevail. Let's face it, who would want to work there?

This will leave you and many others feeling demotivated and disengaged. The Sunday night feeling where you dread going to work because of your heavy heart will become the norm. The stress levels will rise and, as you struggle to remain optimistic, your relationships will start to suffer. Worst of all, the most important relationship you'll ever have in your life will also start to suffer: the relationship you have with yourself. As the impact of workplace toxicity creeps up, it will take its toll on your mental, emotional, and physical health and, if you have started to feel that way, rest assured that many others will be feeling it too.

Like I said earlier, the cost of not focusing on workplace culture and your people runs into the billions across the globe. But let's remember that the underlying cost runs way deeper than that. It's the cost of human suffering, and nothing in life is worth that.

CASE STUDY: PSS

A shining example of an organisation that is embedding a coaching culture is PSS. A social enterprise that provides outstanding service to communities, helping them to live happy and healthy lives. Nonetheless, to do this well, they need highly engaged and motivated employees, and that's why there's been a focus on culture for several years. This is a story of good to great.

And it started with values. Unlike many organisations, PSS live and breathe their values. They were developed and agreed upon by every member of the organisation. Why? Because at PSS, they work collaboratively, adopting an important principle of 'working with', not 'doing to'. As we know, unfortunately, the latter approach is often the reason behind many a failed change initiative in other organisations.

However, in PSS, the values are so entrenched in the culture, they are regarded even more highly than technical skills. At every one-to-one meeting, examples are discussed of where the values have been demonstrated, and where they haven't. This provides time and space for healthy self-reflection without fear of consequence.

Back in 2020, it was identified that the culture was well on its way to being great. To take the culture to the next level, there needed to be a greater focus on people finding time to reflect and take responsibility for their own development. Essentially that meant developing an organisational growth mindset. The answer to that was a coaching culture.

Historically, at PSS, coaching had been seen as something that addressed poor performance. To change that perception and take the culture to the next level, a more positive coaching strategy had to be implemented. People who were interested in learning how to coach came forward and a series of training sessions took place. While coaching capability was growing in the organisation, it was felt that there was more still needed to sustain the development.

PSS knew that we provided affordable digital solutions that could help to keep the learnings alive and change behaviours for the long term. Because of this, we arranged to meet up to have a deeper conversation.

I made the short trip down the M62 and headed into Liverpool to meet with the People and Finance Director and the Head of Learning and Development. We instantly hit it off with our mutual love for coaching as we'd all personally experienced the impact. Just as importantly, we knew that coaching could be both fun and accessible. It didn't need to be seen as some dark art reserved for a select few anymore.

I shared our innovative digital solutions as I knew they would be able to support their coaching strategy and the ambition to develop a coaching culture. They were delighted at how fresh, modern and professional our approach to coaching and self-coaching was. We shared stories of how the coaching industry needed to be modernised, and how engaging digital solutions could help with that.

Not long after that, our digital solutions were launched alongside several other coaching initiatives to develop their people. Just like when a stone is thrown into a pond, as more and more people started to enjoy the benefits, the ripple effect of positive change began.

At PSS, the drum is constantly being beaten about the power of coaching. It's brought into CPD sessions with the digital solutions being part of the agenda, and video clips of success stories are widely shared as more and more people thrive on the difference it makes.

As the saying goes, 'the proof is in the pudding'. At PSS, as this is such an important strategic objective with a clear focus, they now produce an annual coaching report. The evidence of success is there for all to see. Just one example is how the dial moved in 2022 on the confidence score, from 54% of people feeling confident to 99%. A phenomenal achievement in anyone's book.

It's important to the senior team at PSS that the solutions are accessible to everyone, that the team feel valued and ultimately feel better about themselves. One of the greatest secrets to the PSS success is that it's driven by the Exec team at the top. So much so, Sharon Edwards, the Director of People & Finance, knew that coaching needed to be role-modelled from the top, so she became a professionally accredited coach. The Exec team are clear that taking PSS from good to great hasn't happened overnight. Like the flywheel effect described in Jim Collins' book *Good to Great*, developing any great culture takes continuous effort over time.

The Exec team at PSS are formidable human beings who care deeply about their employees and the communities they serve. Like Eleanor Rathbone, the PSS founder 100 years previous, not only do they passionately believe in people, but they also make things happen.

To top it all off, PSS won 'Coaching Culture of the Year' at our prestigious awards ceremony back in 2022. A true winner in all the judges' eyes. And if the evening's celebrations are anything to go by, the team seemed more than delighted with this honour too.

> *"The team at Coaching Culture are human. They just get it. They are experts who take a fresh approach, and they listen to our needs."*

Sharon Edwards, Director of People and Finance, PSS

Working with PSS is an absolute joy. To work with an organisation that has a true purpose to make such a difference to the lives of so many resonates deep within my heart.

WHAT TO DO

Step 1: Assess your coaching culture on an on-going basis

Just because you think you've developed a winning culture, it doesn't mean you can rest on your laurels and stop there. Culture is a never-ending journey. New people join the organisation and others leave. Things change and that's OK. It needs constant nurturing.

Imagine the organisation is like a huge garden. Seeds are sown. New flowers and shrubs are planted while the dead ones removed. They all need feeding and watering. All of this takes time to blossom. It's never quite the finished article. It's a constant work-in-progress.

So is your coaching culture.

It's important to regularly review the climate of the organisation, checking in with what people are thinking and feeling. This allows you to keep on top of what is being said and nip any issues in the bud. Not only that, but it also allows you to move from good to great, like in the case of PSS. A coaching culture must be regularly reviewed through ongoing feedback and employee surveys.

Building your surveys to measure the essentials of a coaching culture can assess the following:

1. How many managers have the capability to coach?

2. How self-aware are managers?

3. How well are managers role-modelling the desired behaviours?

4. How effective are coaching conversations?

5. How frequently are coaching conversations happening?

6. How much is feedback part of everyday life?

7. How effectively is performance being managed and measured?

8. How are coaching conversations being rewarded and recognised?

When coaching conversations are embedded into the fabric of the organisation, and coaching becomes the air that you breathe, the following results will start to shine through:

Outcome

1. Talent attraction and retention

2. Employee engagement

3. Customer satisfaction

4. Wellbeing

5. Inclusivity

6. Creativity and innovation

7. Trust and psychological safety

8. Financial performance

Step 2: Role model what great looks like

Role modelling the expected skills and behaviours is essential to success. It's important that managers not only say the right thing to their teams, but they act in the right way too. There's nothing worse than seeing a manager saying one thing but doing another.

In a coaching culture, managers must have the confidence and capability to have coaching conversations and be able to give and receive feedback. Not only that, but they should role model the use of any technology that supports the management of performance and celebrate the successes as a result.

And there's more.

Managers need to be supported to continually raise their own self-awareness, show care and empathy for their teams and be able to develop their teams to be the best they can be.

There needs to be a constant reinforcement of what great looks like. Managers need to be role-modelling the building of trust, asking questions, listening with intent, creating accountability in others, giving and receiving feedback.

Providing time to reflect on what's working and what's not on a frequent basis will allow greater self-awareness, both on an individual and team basis. A good way to do this is by writing thoughts and reflections down in a journal. It's a proven technique to help people to change their perspective, achieve goals and develop even further. Often just slowing down to think allows progress to speed up in so many areas.

Powerful reflection questions:

1.   What went well?

2.   What didn't go as well?

3.   What needs to change for next time?

Step 3: Celebrate successes and recognise great work

It takes time and effort to regularly water and feed a garden to nurture it into full bloom. Likewise, it takes time and effort to build a coaching culture. And like any beautiful garden, it's worth it. It requires constant effort and attention, meaning that you need to show drive, dedication and motivation in what you do. No wonder it's important to stop, pause and reflect on successes.

Celebrating the wins along the way, no matter how great or small, is proven to release the feel-good hormone, dopamine, into the brain. It builds confidence and reinforces the great work that has been achieved.

Some of the best organisations, who are achieving real success in this area, showcase and celebrate the many wins gained through great coaching conversations. This often includes video testimonials and dedicated awards at the organisational awards ceremonies.

As the word gets out, and more people hear the good news stories, it's inevitable that more people will want to reap the benefits of coaching conversations and get their name on a trophy.

Constant communication of what is expected, role modelling great conversations and reinforcing the expected behaviours, will embed and sustain the coaching culture. The more successes you can celebrate, the more your organisation will truly grow, thrive and perform to the highest level.

EXERCISE: TIME FOR MANAGER FEEDBACK

The purpose of this exercise is to assess how well your managers are role-modelling the desired behaviours.

1. Design the feedback survey to assess the desired behaviours linked to the values, coaching capability levels, how they give and receive feedback and how they manage performance.

2. Engage the management population about the feedback process, answering any questions or concerns that may arise.

3. Ask the managers to nominate who they would like to receive feedback from, ensuring a wide range of people are included, to get the most balanced feedback. Seek a range of relationships, at different levels, capturing different observations; it's not an exercise to just ask the people who they get on with the most.

4. Send the feedback exercise out to the nominated people, explaining clearly what is expected of them, and how to give the feedback.

5. When the feedback is in, and a feedback report is created, it's always recommended to set up a coaching session to coach them through the feedback, the comments, observations, and next steps.

HEAD TO JOWRIGHT.COM
TO DOWNLOAD MORE RESOURCES

TOP TEN TAKEAWAYS

In this chapter, we have learned:

1. A coaching culture is a place where authentic leaders and managers help people to grow, thrive and perform through effective conversations and honest feedback, underpinned by trust.

2. A healthy culture and workplace is the way to succeed in the 21st century.

3. There are no downsides to a coaching culture.

4. People flourish in a coaching culture.

5. Personal development and growth are evident in a coaching culture.

6. Teams collaborate well in a coaching culture.

7. Responsibility and accountability shifts in a coaching culture.

8. To embed a coaching culture, managers must role model the desired behaviours.

9. Building a coaching culture requires effort, grit and determination.

10. To sustain a coaching culture, it needs constant effort, re-evaluation, role-modelling of behaviours and celebration of successes.

CHAPTER 12

GETTING STARTED

YOU'RE ON YOUR WAY

C ongratulations!

By choosing to read this book, and taking the time to do so, you've taken the all-important first step towards building a coaching culture. You've read within the pages of this book that it is possible to achieve.

By now, you should have gathered inspiration, valuable insight, tools and resources and, most importantly, you should have developed your own confidence and belief to know that you too are now fully equipped to make work better.

It's always worth remembering that if others can do it, so can you!

I'm delighted to say that you can now:

1. Influence your senior leaders to invest in building a coaching culture.

2. Create a clear coaching culture strategy.

3. Engage the wider business to win hearts and minds.

4. Enable your managers to build their confidence and capability to have coaching conversations.

5. Unlock the power of coaching and feedback in the organisation.

6. Ensure performance is managed through everyday conversations.

7. Celebrate successes and embed a coaching culture.

NEXT STEPS

To get you started, please do head over to jowright.com to download the workbook and get access to Coaching Culture's resources and tools. You will find a host of powerful downloadable resources and inspiration, such as the seven step framework, more case studies, webinars and ready-made programmes.

You may already be itching to take your organisation to another level and ready to join the growing number of successful organisations who are already on this journey. If that's the case, then why not upgrade to our premium tools and resources as they've all been created to help you succeed.

To give you comfort to know that you're not alone on this journey, feel free to take a look at what others are saying.

WHAT OTHERS ARE SAYING

"Coaching Culture's Mindset modules gave us the opportunity to enhance our offering for personal development and self-coaching as well as great tools for our internal coaches. We now also use Coaching Lessons to enhance our coaching capability across the business."

Sarah Draycott, Talent Partner, Warburtons

"The feedback from colleagues about the Great Conversations programme has been amazing. In fact, because of colleague word of mouth, places were snapped up quicker than Peter Kay tickets."

**Kerry Ogden, People Development Partner,
Great Places Housing Group**

"People love the Coaching Culture products, and we love our relationship. It's a great partnership, and very pioneering for the Middle East."

**Andrew Stotter-Brooks, Former Vice President of
Learning & Development, Etihad Aviation Group**

"When I was at Motorpoint, I chose to use a blended learning approach with the Coaching Culture materials to establish a confident and competent coaching culture across the company. It was important to me that coaching was understood at all levels and used naturally

in conversations as well as in more focused situations such as performance or personal support. I would highly recommend using Coaching Culture to truly establish a culture of coaching across your business."

Emma Wilson-Wyer, Former Head of Learning & Development, Motorpoint

"Following research into scalable solutions that could be accessed anywhere and at any time, we came across Coaching Culture. We were so impressed by Lessons and Mindset, as well as the ability to easily integrate them into our existing LMS, that we chose Coaching Culture as our partner to help us drive a coaching culture across our organisation."

Andrea Naylor, Senior Manager, Learning & Development, Etihad Aviation Group

"The resources on offer contain a great variety of content which has helped to support an increase in engagement in self-coaching across many teams. The impact of this can be evidenced by personal and team development. The Coaching Culture team pay attention to every detail, are very proactive and maintain strong customer relations. They deliver a consistent, reliable and friendly approach."

Nicola Walker, HR Partner, Edge Hill University

"Coaching Culture are a true L&D partner. They've been instrumental in supporting us create a coaching based culture that brings coaching, feedback and reflection to not only the way people learn but everyday conversations in our business."

Adam Evans,
Learning Technologist Specialist, Currys

"On our journey to embrace how we lead with a coach mindset, we are really excited to be partnering with Coaching Culture. The fabulous suite of content and solutions will help us democratise coaching by giving leaders the ability to coach themselves and others."

Carol Campbell, Retail Director, Major Home
Improvement Retailer

"The Coaching Culture content is great for any organisation looking to empower their workforce to make a positive change, through the power of coaching."

Edwina Quansah, Employee Engagement & Talent
Business Partner, Coventry City Council

"Through the help of the team at Coaching Culture, we have made real progress into shifting the mindset of our leaders and started to create a coaching culture…"

Matt Davis, Organisational Developer,
University of Liverpool

"The Coaching Culture modules have given all our staff the opportunity to access personal and self-development at their own leisure and they have been empowered to select the most appropriate modules to meet their learning needs. As an organisation this complements the ongoing development of embedding a coaching culture across our Trust to improve staff personal and professional development ultimately improving patient care."

Julia Ford, OD Practitioner/ Coaching Lead, North Staffordshire Combined Health Care NHS Trust

"We have always been struck by the quality and engaging nature of the Coaching Culture solutions and were just waiting for the right opportunity to work with the team. We are excited to see where it will take us on our journey to becoming a 'Learning Organisation' with coaching at its heart."

Donna Warr, Head of Organisational Capability, Stonewater

"Coaching Culture supports our mission to create a teamwork culture where everyone feels valued and supported. Coaching Culture has great tools for team members to use to self-develop by learning coaching techniques and effective communication. Personal development is enhanced through self-awareness modules and interactive online lessons which we use in groups and individually."

Nora Jones, Head of Learning and Development, NewFlex

"Working with Coaching Culture will help us embed our own coaching culture within Toshiba Group throughout EMEA and we are excited to see the difference this makes as we start on our journey."

Ian Robinson, Senior Manager, Corporate HR & Administration, (EMEA), Toshiba

"Working with the team at Coaching Culture, I have to say I have been, and continue to be, super impressed with the whole team's desire and willingness to engage, adapt and support us on our coaching journey. Their practical approach to coaching enablement, content, delivery, and support has been inspiring as we strive to build our own 'army of coaches'."

Stephen Fowler, EMEA Sales Coach, UiPath

CONNECT WITH ME

Now it would be a shame to just leave it there. So, let's stay connected and continue this journey together.

You can find me on LinkedIn or contact me through my website jowright.com. I'll always love to hear your stories, how you're making work better or how this book may have inspired you in some way.

The more we spread the word, the more we will collectively make work better. So if you know of others who want to make a difference, then why not share this book and talk about your learnings and experiences? And in the spirit of the book, why not share your feedback on Amazon?

Finally, please make sure to keep a look out for any forthcoming events or talks I may be doing, where we can stay connected and meet with other like-minded people who are wanting to make the world of work a better place.

ONE FINAL QUESTION

Ok, so let me leave you with these final thoughts.

Remember my mum's inspiring words from the first page of the book?

'There's no such word as can't.'

Well, while you reflect on her words, let me ask you one final coaching question:

What are you waiting for?

REFERENCES

I love a great book, and I've been inspired by many fabulous authors throughout my career. I've referred to a small selection of those books and research papers in this book.

Here they are as an easy reminder if you want to check them out.

- Breathe H.R, *The Culture Economy* report, 2021

- C.I.P.D, *Health and Wellbeing* report, 2022

- Caspar Craven, *Be More Human*, 2020

- Jim Collins, *Good to Great*, 2001

- Michael Bungay Stanier, *The Coaching Habit*, 2016

- Stephen Covey, *The 7 Habits of Highly Effective People*, 1989

FURTHER READING

I f, like me, you love to learn, and love a good book recommendation, here are some more of my favourite books that have influenced me throughout my career.

- Brené Brown, *Dare to Lead*

- Dr Carol Dweck, *Mindset*

- Charles Duhigg, *The Power of Habit*

- Daniel Coyle, *The Culture Code*

- Daniel Goleman, *Emotional Intelligence*

- David Liddle, *Transformational Culture*

- Geoff Watts & Kim Morgan, *The Coach's Casebook*

- Greg McKeown, *Essentialism*

- James Clear, *Atomic Habits*

- Matthew Michalewicz, *Life in Half a Second*

- Matthew Syed, *Black Box Thinking*

- Phil Knight, *Shoe Dog*

- Reed Hastings & Erin Meyer, *No Rules Rules*

- Simon Sinek, *Start With Why*

ACKNOWLEDGEMENTS

I am grateful to many people who have influenced me to be who I am today and been part of my journey so far. The book is based upon decades of real-world experience and invaluable learnings, for which I will be forever grateful.

I would like to specifically thank the following people for the part they have played in the creation of this book.

FAMILY AND FRIENDS

My husband, Graham. For allowing me to read this book out loud, word by word, line by line, chapter by chapter. Your words of encouragement in the writing of this book and your unending patience at my 5am starts has been exactly what I needed to get this done.

My dad. For teaching me to be hard-working, kind-hearted and grateful to be alive every day. I hope you love this book, in spite of the cheeky title. I know how much you dislike swear words!

My big brother, Gary. For your constant encouragement, for the fact that you never, ever doubt me and for being one of my greatest cheerleaders. It's happening!

My step-sister-in-law, Liz Lakin, who passed away less than one year before the writing of this book began. I think about you every day. When I listen to the song 'My Silver Lining' by First Aid Kit, I feel your love and encouragement shining down on me, and because of you, I will always keep on keeping on.

Tim Roberts, author of *Break the Mould* and long-time friend of Coaching Culture. Without you, Tim, I'm not sure I would have known how to start putting pen to paper. You showed me the way. You introduced me to Leila and Ali, and you gave me the self-belief that writing a book was absolutely possible.

Maxine Mayhew and Simon Kilby. For always being there to listen and to encourage, and for inspiring me to push myself further in life.

Sam and Toby Windsor. For allowing me to get the creative juices flowing from the beautiful and peaceful surrounds of your garden.

COACHING CULTURE TEAM

Adam Kara. Who knows what I would be doing now if I'd not gate-crashed my way onto your course? Thank you for pushing me out of my comfort zone.

Sinead Brown, Emma Denton, Tom Dunman, Steph Durbin, Jude Hallam, Laura Hayes, Emily Jones, Kim Kara, Justyna Kowalski, Donald McIntosh, Rob Moors, Steve Poulton, Tim Roberts, Natalie Stewart, Anthony Taylor, Debbie Thomas and Sharon Woods.

Thank you all for being an essential part of the Coaching Culture journey. You have made this book a reality.

BOOK COACHES

Leila Green and Ali Dewji, from Get-Known Publishing. 'When the student is ready, the teacher will appear'. How very true. Thank you both for coaching me through this book, every step of the way.

Henry Harding and Ben Watkins. For helping me to add the sparkle and glitter to take my first ever book to market.

LOYAL CUSTOMERS AND SUPER-FANS

To all our loyal customers and super-fans. You are helping to deliver on the purpose to make work better, believing in the solutions and helping to make the world of work a better place. For this, I will be forever grateful.

In particular, thank you to the following people for taking the time to share your stories, your case studies and testimonials. I cannot thank you enough.

Carol Campbell (Major Retailer), Matt Davies (University of Liverpool), Sarah Draycott (Warburtons PLC), Sharon Edwards (PSS), Adam Evans (Currys), Julia Ford (North Staffordshire Combined Health Care NHS Trust), Stephen Fowler (UiPath), Louisa Fryer (Restore PLC), Nora Jones (NewFlex), Emma Lidgett (Kainos Group), Lizi Marsden (Great Places Housing Group), Andrea Naylor (Etihad Aviation Group), Kerry Ogden (Great Places Housing Group), Edwina Quansah (Coventry City Council), Michelle Reid (Institute of Occupational Medicine), Ian Robinson (Toshiba), Andrew Stotter-Brooks (formerly of Etihad Aviation Group), Lucy Scally (Impellam PLC), Joanne Scott (Government Agency), Rob Smyth (formerly of Silva Homes), Nicola Walker (Edge Hill University), Donna Warr (Stonewater), Lin Watson (Silva Homes), Emma Wilson-Wyer (formerly of Motorpoint).

LINKEDIN FRIENDS AND INFLUENCERS

To my LinkedIn friends, followers, mentors and coaches. Thank you for your constant words of encouragement, for pushing me forwards, for being my cheerleaders and for keeping me real. I couldn't do this without you. A special thank you must go to Martin Baker, Mike Bedford, Graham Carter, Caspar Craven, Helen Dann, Jules Darvill, Wendy Doherty, Susie Finch, Michelle Hartley, Indy Lachhar, Nicholé McGill-Higgins, Kim Morgan, Steve Nestor, Joe Noya, Paul Phelan, Jules Roberts, Kelly Swingler and Perry Timms.

Printed in Great Britain
by Amazon